What Color is a Butterfly

What Color is a Butterfly

A Biography of a Blind Girl

GRACE HUDLOW ODELL

To order additional copies of this book, contact:
Xlibris Corporation
1-888-795-4274
www.Xlibris.com
Orders@Xlibris.com
15449

Contents

PREFACE

Both in my growing years and my adult life I listened to my mother's tales of her life at the "blind school". She drew verbal pictures of the "school" and the people there as we sat with her on the porch swing or around her rocking chair next to the fireplace. What I can't adequately discribe here is the smug grin of satisfaction on her face as she discribed the pleasure in her mischief. When she died her grandchildren and those yet to be born would miss knowing about some of the great times in her life and her mischief, so I wanted to record some of the interesting details of her life. Therefore, upon starting this project I undertook to read extensively about novel writing, about "voice", the pros and cons of successful writers and their books. I took a writing class with an editor at my local newspaper and went to seminars around California. I selected an editor who is a best selling novelist and worked with her until she continued to complain about points in my books that were "unrealistic" but were in fact, true. When necessary, I studied, most recently a relatively new science called "Echo Location," now known for its use in sonar technology but those who knew Ruth will be the first to say that was one of her gifts.

I interviewed ship's staff from Denmark, medical doctors of obstetrics, ophthalmology and pharmacology as well as many others in general medicine. In Little Rock I visited the Arkansas School for the Blind, interviewed the present Superintendent who gave me access to the school's archives and visited the site of the old school where both my parents went to school. (The structures have been replaced with a new governor's mansion formerly occupied by President and Mrs.Clinton when he was Arkansas's governor.) I read books by Helen Keller about her life.* I visited the historical section of the North Little Rock public library. (North Little Rock was formerly Arjenta.) I spoke to the Archivist at the school of medicine in St. Louis, the former site of the school of osteopathic medicine. I can't begin to count the number of blind citizens I interviewed, some elderly who knew my mother while she was in school, others were musicians of fine ability and ear training, one a teacher from the California School for the Blind, blind children as young as five and others who were willing to relate their fears, inner feelings and their experiences to me, a total stranger.

I am deeply grateful to all those who have shared with me for the purpose of writing this book. Most of the family members completed my questionnaire and gave me very useful information. Sometimes those were in conflict with other's information. I sorted out to the best of my ability which was true and if at all possible worked their stories into this book. Dr. Fred and Mrs. Virginia Henker were of willing and invaluable help making contact with the blind community in Little Rock and in otherwise getting me to the best sources for the information I needed in Arkansas.

To all who wrote or spoke to me about this project, please accept my deepest gratitude

Fresno, California
January 9, 2002

Grace Hudlow Odell

---

* Helen Keller was a guest of honor for the opening of the new Arkansas School for the Blind in the late 50's.

CHAPTER ONE

Dr. Lindgren

She lay on the table in Doc Lindren's office, fretful at the bright, white light above or, perhaps, at just being moved from the warmth and comfort of my shoulder. In a way, I wanted to keep her on my shoulder, not to relinquish her to the examining table, as if not knowing about her eye condition was preferable to bad news. Most certainly the news would be bad. How could it be otherwise? Oh sure, the eyelids of all newborns were a little red and swollen for a week or so. Ruth's were certainly that and more. They were sick eyes similar to an infection. The brown crustiness locked her top lid to the lower lid. Even Peter couldn't open her eyes. Peter mentioned it was like the scabbing on a knee that took a sliding fall in the dirt. Doc Lindgren was over her, mumbling a little, turning to hum a tune with no melody. He put drops of clear liquid, waited a minute and pulled the right eyelid open and stared intently into the eyeball. He stopped his tune for only a second, a split second. What did his silence mean?

Then he resumed his hum as he moved over to the left eye. Again, he stopped abruptly. I detected a slight headshake, a jerk to the right, a jerk to he left, just once but it was there. His brow furrowed, ever so lightly. He stopped for a few seconds as he concentrated, returned his eyeglasses to his nose with one hand and pulled off his mirrored lens with the other. He hadn't looked at any other part of her body, just the eyes. He scooped up our Ruth and turned to hand her to her father, his eyes avoiding both

Peter's and mine. He took a deep breath and settled against the examining table, taking his time to empty all the air from his lungs.

The casualness of his hum renewed my hope. Then I caught the hesitancy in the hum. I was afraid.

"There is no easy way to say this, so I'll just be about as frank as I know how to be," he began, "your baby is virtually blind."

There it was. It was cold. It was blunt. It hit like a packed snowball right between the eyes, hard and painful. It was the confrontation, the ensnarement, and the guillotine. Even though I really had known in my heart of its almost certain probability, I had to hope. Oh, did I hope! I felt stunned as if struck by a bolt of lightning, numb and unable to speak. This hypnotic state-e-e . . . . ug-g-g.

I don't remember what happened. Suddenly, it began to grow dark and my body transformed into a cooked onion ring. The next thing I remember I was on the floor, with Peter on his knees beside me. Cradled in his left arm was our baby but the warm palm of his other hand held my hand. He just looked at me, more moisture that usual in his eyes, as he gently moved his thumb over my palm. In a hazy distance, I could hear Doc Lindgren saying. "She's just fainted. She'll be all right. Give her a little air."

Someone put my feet up on a footstool. I looked at Peter, the moisture on his lower lids, a mild quiver in his lower lip. I saw Ruth in his arms and I began to hear the words again, those dreaded words spoken a few short minutes before.

"Your baby is virtually blind."

That statement was my worst fear. I almost knew it when we came in the door but I couldn't allow myself to consider it a reality. The reality was at the door but I bolted the door, I braced the door as if my efforts could stop what already WAS. Rejection set in. "How can I teach a baby that doesn't see? What kind of life can she have? What kind of future?"

If anyone heard my questions they didn't respond. Very softly, Peter said, "Lillemor, there's nothing in this whole wide world you and I cannot handle together. I'm here with you. You and I, together, will make the best of this situation."

And then the tears came. As if the floor-gates opened, I couldn't help myself. I just cried. Quietly the tears flowed, channeling into rivulets down the temples of my head, my hair acting like a sponge to handle the overflow of sorrow.

Doc Lindgren cautioned. "Just stay where you are, for the time being. You can sit up, though, if you wish. Slow-w-ly." He continued. "Steady, my dear. You've been carrying a big load of a child for many months now.

Your wagon's overloaded as a wife and mother of a family of children, and now you've got a still bigger load to carry."

He paused as he inhaled deeply and slowly let all the air from his lungs, as if looking for his next words. "But I know you and I know your stock. You've made your way in this country because of your strength and you'll make the best of this situation just like you've managed before."

As he spoke, I'm not sure how much of what he said registered in my brain, but gradually I felt better, and with Peter's help, moved up to a chair. Peter thanked Doc Lindgren for his consideration and kindness.

Doc Lindgren continued, "Ruth will have light into her eyes, which means she will be able to pick out some lines, perhaps, images, perhaps some colors. But how much will be in question for several years." As he spoke, he made direct eye contact first with me and then Peter, as though he was looking straight through our eyes to see the flash of "HELP" messaged on our brains. I liked Doc Lindgren. I trusted him. I felt he was about the best doctor we could ever have.

"You see, the eyes are like windows and since I'm not inside looking out through those windows, I can't tell exactly how much dirt or scarring is there but the damage is major and irreversible. Expect a complete loss of sight and be surprised if she can see anything at all. We'll have to wait for Ruth to grow and determine that for herself."

He sat down in his wooden swivel chair, folded his arms across his chest and continued in his grandfatherly manner, and slowly and thoughtfully proceeded.

"Your child is not the first, you know. In fact serious eye damage at birth is quite common, I hate to say. And I know you may not consider this possibility at this time, but it could be worse you know, much worse. Other accidents and diseases have produced blind people into our midst for centuries, and thank the good Lord, now as we're almost into the 20th century and attitudes are beginning to change.

Block out all the old wives' tales about blindness being contagious, or that you, her parents, are being punished for your sins. Or that the God's are seeking vengeance against you or her. That's poppycock. Pure RUBBISH!"

Peter spoke up. "You mentioned changes. What changes are you speaking of?"

"I'll get to that in a minute, Peter," and then he continued. "Some of us are still not completely clear on this subject of what affliction there is, actually. Why, just last week I was sitting next to Maggard, the barber's brother. He's blind, you know. I was at 'Sadie's Diner' and Sadie asked me what Maggard wanted to order. It was like Maggard was deaf. I told Sadie how would I know. "Ask Maggard. Not me." His voice rose to the preposterous situation. He shook his head and began again. "We've all heard of our Blind Asylums in this country. And in Europe and Asia. Those are dumping grounds, places of incarceration so society doesn't have to SEE them. When Ruth's eyes were burned none of her other senses were effected. I expect she can smell and hear, feel and think. The brain functions, of course. And that's where you come in. Teach her everything you know. Send her to the best specialty schools you know and give her the best opportunities you can afford. She could really surprise you. The best school that I know of, in the United States, that is, is the Perkins Institute in Boston. Their students can learn to read by a relatively new system. They call it Braille."

Fixing his eyes on Peter, "This is what I was referring to. Blind people can now read. They read with their fingers. It's a six point system of dots, each letter of the alphabet having its combination of dots. I hear it's even been modified some in a system for reading music. It's called *New York Point*, I believe. Many blind people excel in music or even in math and the other sciences." Leaning forward he said, almost like he didn't believe it himself. "Did you know a blind man has had the chair in physics in Cambridge, on the recommendation of Sir Isaac Newton, himself?" Most recently, I heard of a young girl who was not only blind but deaf. Not only was she was taught to read but also to write. Can you imagine that? She has developed into an eloquent speaker and a most talented writer, I understand."

"Your task will hardly be easy, for in addition to your daughter's training, you'll have to repeatedly contend with the ignorant and the doubters in our midst. Let me tell you a story to illustrate."

His expression began to change as the laugh lines around his eyes and mouth deepened. "Over in England, there was a very bright blind man who became a fine engineer for their military in India. Also at home. He designed and built roads and bridges. One time he came upon a stranger who was lost in the forest, the forest where he grew up and knew very well. The stranger was unaware of the sight limitations of the chap he had just met on the trail, when he asked for assistance through to the other side. Only on the other edge of the forest did he realize of his guide's *blind* condition."

Doc Lindgren's mouth opened to a smile exposing a missing bicuspid. "Oh Lordy, had I known of your condition, I'd not be paid two pounds Sterling to follow you."

Both of us smiled at his story. He continued.

"Don't decide ahead of time that Ruth is unable to do ANY thing. Know in your own heart that she is bright. Bring her up with confidence and instill that confidence in her. Make her a typical family member participating in the regular chores of the family, with minor adjustments to protect her from harm."

Both of us listened intently to all he had to say. Doc Lindgren was taking a lot of time with us. I relaxed some in his calm and patient voice. Peter was watching me closely and when my eyes met his I felt his love and support.

"Let me know if I can be of any help," and he got up from his chair.

Peter handed me the baby and put out his right hand to shake Doc Lindgren's hand. "Thank you, Doc. I much appreciate you." With that he turned to the door, opened it and ushered me out with our new daughter.

Both of us were very quiet on the ride home from the doctor's office. I held Ruth close so I could keep her warm. Peter had tucked us in well before mounting his side of the buggy for the trip home. The sun was warming. The sparkle it gave the fields and rooftops of snow lifted my spirits a little, although, from time to time, I mopped at a tear.

Two large dogs were playing in the snow on my side of the road. I noticed the smoky breath dipping and circling from their mouths and nostrils, like a wind blown springtime kite. I slid deep into the buggy seat and snuggled beneath my upturned collar. I pulled my stocking cap down to cover my earlobes. As I looked at the snow before me, I thought about the landscape just a few months ago. When the grass was green so were the leaves. Then they shaded into the yellows, reds and browns of the fall, and eventually dropped to the ground. They were still there, somewhere under the snow. The detail in the grass and rooftops was unclear because of the snow covering. The effect of that covering gave nature one of its most awe inspiring pictures. Fall was beautiful with its red and orange leaves. Spring was a new awakening of light green leaves and colorful blossoms, and summer, beautiful in its own way, was different still. Winter was unique, in its own way.

Now the tree trunks are blacker than in the other seasons. It's the same bark but with the dampness of the wet snow, it's darkened to contrast more with the very clean and white, fresh snow. Several bright red cardinals, sitting on the fence railing as we rode past, stood out in sharp contrast against the bright snow. The tiny, yellow-beaked chickadees popped in and out of the trees at the edge of the Brunn farm, lively and spirited.

The snow has fallen on the eyes of my baby. Her eyes are now cloaked in a shroud. She can't see out and I can't see in. Doc Lindgren called it dirt. I see it as snow. The spring will never come for her eyes. She will never see the colors of the maples in the fall. She will always only see snow, white snow."

In the distance I spotted a girl riding horseback. Girl? I questioned. I thought it was a girl by the long hair flowing in the distance. It could have been her hair, or maybe a scarf?

That's something a blind girl could do. If she has good legs and arms she can ride a horse. Why not? There must be many things she can do. We'll teach her. She might do some things better than others. I remembered my own curiosity in watching Peter's helper at the store, the one who had lost a leg fighting for the North in the Civil War. He moved around on a pegged leg as well as the other two legged men in the store. I always watched him because I loved the way he paid no attention to his missing leg and foot. In fact, he used to laugh about it costing him less for shoes because he only had to have one shoe made.

People will stare. They will always stare at anything new or unfamiliar. But it's only because they are not used to them. My tears are gone now. So what they will see in my child will be beauty and accomplishment. There are five of us to help her. Together, we'll all do what I cannot do alone. Together, we'll all raise Ruth.

The horse had slowed and Peter began his turn into the drive leading up to our house. The smoke trailing out into the sky from the chimney reminded me of the warmth underneath that snow-covered roof. This was my warm and happy home, my girls, my life with all its joys and sorrows. There will be better days.

Just inside, my nostrils filled with the smell of the lentil soup with ham I had put on the stove just before leaving for Doc Lindgren's. I handed Ruth to Peter just inside the door and quickly hung my coat on the back of the door. In no time, I opened a jar of canned peaches from last summer's canning, dumped its contents into the metal baking pan and sprinkled them quickly with flour, sugar and cinnamon covering the top. Just before popping it into the oven of the old wood cook stove, I stoked the coals and dropped in another small log. The dessert will be finished baking by the time the biscuits are made and baked.

The family prayer before the evening meal had more significance than before as Peter asked God to, "bless this family, help us to understand what we are to do, give us your direction, guide us with your great wisdom on this the biggest undertaking of our lives. Caress our baby in your loving hands. Be with her always. Take care of all our children, hold us all and, Father, be with us through this day, tomorrow and always. Amen!"

CHAPTER TWO

The Old Country

From the moment Klara's first letter arrived back in Denmark, I knew I had to go too. Everything in the world that was exciting was happening in America. We didn't even know how far it was from our home in Tise but we knew Klara's trip across the ocean took several weeks, so it had to be really far. Only once did I leave home in the upper Jutland Peninsula. We had crossed Lim Fjord on a ferry and gone to Copenhagen. It took us two whole days to get there. Think of how far it must be when it takes weeks to even cross the ocean to get to America. Klara had earlier written that the railroad had now been completed all the way across the United States to San Francisco and that trip took over two weeks of steady traveling.

Every Sunday after services at the Lutheran Church in nearby Ingstrup, our family gathered together for dinner. The women put on aprons over their Sunday's best to complete the meal that had been gently roasting while all were away in church. The Jensen men, Grampa and Papa's other three brothers, looked prim and proper in their Sunday suits but they ate stiffly with their jackets buttoned up. They talked of the prices of butter and cheese, or of their pigs. Always the conversations came around to America and Klara Jensen's letters. Papa loved the attention he got when he began to read her letters to everyone after Mama's apple strudel.

This news was always an important event. Papa's little five foot frame was hard to see so he always stood up, in front of the fireplace as he took the letter out of the envelope. Everyone else quickly stopped their miscellaneous conversations, moved their chairs for a better view of Papa and settled into their positions for alerted hearing.

"Come, let us read what Klara has to say," someone said. Papa would hold the letter in one hand as he stroked his almost white goatee with the other. One Sunday he began to read. About halfway through, he stopped, looked up at his silent listeners as their eyes were transfixed on him and said, "You won't believe next what I am going to tell you."

Uncle Claus looked at Uncle Max with curious expectations.

Papa began to read again. "There is a man in Salt Lake City who took himself sixteen wives."

Uncle Claus stopped him. "How many wives did you say?"

Papa repeated "sixteen" and Uncle Julius called out "Oh-h-wee-ee."

"Oh lorda, lorda" exclaimed Uncle Claus almost at the same time.

"They all live together in the same house?" questioned Uncle Max.

"Did she say how many children there were already?" called out Aunt Trina, in her piercing voice. Everyone talked at the same time.

"Quiet, please. I shall answer your questions with time," Papa raised his hand to quiet them.

"They all live together and several of the women were with child at the same time."

Several gasps came from the women. "How many are there now? Did she say?

"No, not exactly. But lots of children. That's just what she said. 'Lots of children'," nodding with assurance.

Gramma, having been calmly absorbing the drama, softly called out her doubt from her cushioned seat in the window. "They cost too much. How could he afford so many children?"

"What about the opportunities for them all when they grow up?" asked Uncle Julius.

Uncle Claus leaned back on the hard wooden bench, clasped his hands behind his neck, his eyes laughed slightly as he turned to Uncle Julius.

"I can't manage one woman. I'd die an early death with SIXTEEN," said Papa.

Uncle Julius, by now in a full blown smile, "Oh sure, you'd die an early death but we'd see a mighty big smile on your face as you laid in your resting place."

Their bodies shook with laughter. I watched Grampa's smiling face, enjoying the remark, but he got serious again right away. "Those people are all part of the Mormon religion. They believe that to be God's way."

Gentle and understanding Papa spoke next. "Having so many children makes many converts for the church. It grows big and strong and that's good. Each man must follow his own convictions. If it's Mormonism or Lutheranism, each of us can reach into our hearts and be honest with our souls."

To me, it seemed to be too many people to cook for, to wash for. But, no matter, in my own mind I was already planning to follow in Klara's footsteps to America when I finished at the country school in Borglum. I was so lucky to have a sister already over there. Klara told me what to do and even made the arrangements for a family to sponsor me.

It wasn't easy to move to America. One didn't just decide to go there. It seemed everybody wanted to go to America. Not so many coming from Denmark, though. You wouldn't believe what I had to go through, just like the examinations of a horse before he went to auction. They looked at my teeth and checked my eyes from a hot-breath distance. I didn't have to undress for the doctor but he pressed every spot on my body, listening, feeling and asking a lot of questions before writing a letter saying I didn't have any diseases. And he talked to Mama about our family history. I filled out a big questionnaire about my political beliefs. Klara told me what to write.

The wait for a reply was endless, or at least it seemed so. I was beginning to think my application had gotten lost in the mail and then it finally came. The village postman in Borglum rode his horse for the delivery of this special letter from the Office of Emigration in Washington, D.C. He knew it must be important. In it was my passport, my passport to America. It was in my full name of Johanna Marie Jensen, born in Tise Sogn on July 6, 1857. I was now 16 years old. All plans were carefully put together by early spring of 1873. Shortly after the first of May, the time had come to begin my journey.

When I left the only home I'd ever known, the snow was still under the bushes up on the hills and on the north side of the trees. But the fields on the west side of the barn were covered in yellow and white wild flowers, honeysuckle and hyacinth. Each time I walked out the door it was just like opening the drawer filled with mama's wonderful pot pourri of dried flowers.

"Mama, you hate those pesky flowers when they're out in the fields but you like them in your bouquets."

"Yes, yes, they push out my vegetables. I can't pull enough of them. They just keep coming back." Mama swished around the kitchen in her long black skirt.

They weren't pests to me this morning as they stretched their faces toward the sun. Papa and Otto, the hired man, loaded up the old steamer trunk we had purchased from a lady in the village. Mama's warm quilt sewn and quilted by her own hands almost filled the trunk and did with my few clothes added. She insisted I needed a basket of "nourishment" for the trip, too. It included a big hunk of Gammel Ole cheese, dried fruit and several strips of dried codfish.

Bulder, Papa's big brown dog danced and pranced around in excitement. Something was in the air. Mama was waiting to feed him until just before we were to leave, so he wouldn't be so likely to follow us. I would miss old Bulder. He had been in our family for 12 years now, chasing rabbits on the hill, following Papa's plow in the field, and he seemed always to be at the kitchen door, no matter when we opened it. He won't be here too many more years, I thought.

"Don't forget, we got to stop in Borglum to Thompson's boot-making shop for her new shoes," she reminded Papa.

"Ya, ya! I don't forget the important matters."

Mama then turned to me. "Your grandfather makes good shoes. They're a special pair for you to take to America. You won't need another pair for many years. Remember to thank him," she reminded me.

"I know, Mama. I've thanked him already last Sunday when I said 'Goodbye' to him."

"Good! Good! You'll do fine in America."

Out of the house for the last time, I turned to shake Otto's hand just before I climbed into the wagon. "Goodbye, Otto."

"Goodbye, Miss Johanna," he said, his slightly stooped back showing signs of arthritis. His head dipped in respect. He'd never done that before. For nine years he'd worked for Papa and he was always polite but this time he gave an awkward bow, like when the Queen passed by.

As Papa pulled the wagon out from the opening between the stone fences of our property, the land smelled of spring, still wet and fresh. Today, I don't even mind the smells of the barnyard, I thought. It smells like home. I smiled at the thought of my home smelling like the manure of the cow pen but then settled into the moment of leaving my home probably forever. I'll never smell this again, or see the spring of Tise or Borglum. I should have gathered two or three of those little flowers to take with me. I'd keep them fresh as long as I could and then press them in my Bible. Never mind, now, it's too late.

I watched the fields of knee high grass as it rippled in the breeze when we passed. Sometimes there were grazing reindeer, stopping to cast a suspicious eye at our moving wagon. There were all those Sunday afternoons that we spread out one of Mama's quilts on the hillside covered with the tall grass. I thought of the way we would bury ourselves in its height, lying on our backs and watching the sky as we dreamed of things to come, of a life to come. The grass rippled in the wind and looked much like the very gentle waves I had seen in the waters of Lim Fjord. We had some wonderful afternoons lying on the hillside. Tiny little birds gathered over us, stopping in flight, suspended directly over us. They sang as though they were performing just for us.

Not in my wildest dreams did I ever think about going away so far from home, to America. I was now leaving all this beauty, all chances of racing across the fields in the sunlight with the wind whipping my long blond hair. As I watched the land move past our wagon, I knew I would never see this sight again. In a way I wanted Papa to slow down so I could examine every detail of these scenes, but the boat wouldn't wait for me. I tried to record every small thing my eyes would cover. As long as the wagon kept the view, my eyes nourished in the picture before me.

"You remember Lilla's address?" Mama interrupted, half turning from the seat next to Papa.

"Yes, Mama."

"How about Grampa Thompson and Grandma Jensen's?"

"Yes, yes, yes. Don't worry, we haven't forgotten anything."

Mama's attention was caught as she turned to follow a fox, racing for cover in the briar bushes. We both were quiet for a moment as we continued to watch the bush. I wished the fox would come out again.

"Where did you pack the cameo Papa and I gave you last Christmas?" Without waiting for an answer, she called to Papa to "Slow down! Wait for her chicks to cross." Papa had already slowed to miss the line of quail, as we rounded a hill.

I didn't answer. I knew she forgot the question and was just making conversation again. She became silent again, for quite a while. She pulled out a white handkerchief to dab her eyes. It should have been easier, for this second time a daughter of hers left home for a far-away place. I guess it's always hard for a mother to say goodbye to her youngest, her baby.

Our road paralleled the sea for a while, but when we turned in toward the coast the water came into our view, I leaned forward to get a better look. Papa turned his head to the side so neither of his ladies would see his face. He was always so strong and solid. We gathered our strength from him. Could it be, at this time when his youngest was leaving forever that he was beginning to crumble?

For five miles the road ran through sand dunes. We watched the houses and buildings of the port town slowly grow larger as our wagon got closer. Mama inhaled deeply as she rearranged her carriage blanket against the chill in the air coming off the great North Sea. Papa became more attentive as we neared the series of joined buildings and onto the cobblestone streets that made up the town. Very gradually, he slowed for the townspeople and activities around the open shops.

The first stop was Grandpa Thompson's. The shoes were waiting for me and were just what I wanted. As Papa talked to him about the weather in the channel yesterday, I put on the new shoes, leaving the badly worn pair on the floor for him to leave out for one of the drifters always hanging around the city.

At the end of the town we approached the dock and the berth where the fishing boat that was to take me to London, sat low in the water heavy with fish for the British market. I felt the eyes of several of the men on the dock, as they stopped their work to turn and watch us. We got out of the wagon and Papa began to pull out my trunk when two men appeared to help him.

Sailors working on the dock stopped to look at us as I stepped from the wagon. They carried my steamer trunk and the smaller case aboard right away. I hung onto the food basket, myself. Mama's tears were already rolling down her face. She kept touching her cheeks with her handkerchief. "Long good-byes are hard on everyone and not at all necessary," proclaimed Papa. We hugged. I turned away and walked up the gangway, hanging onto my skirt as the wind whipped up my dark wool cape. We put my things in the cabin where the steering wheel was. Just inside, I dropped my basket and went back to waive to Mama and Papa. Too late! They were already back in the wagon and moving away from the dock. But as I watched, I could see Mama turn to look back just as their wagon turned from sight at the end of the storage sheds.

It wasn't long before my eye caught sight of a man at dock's edge. He was untying our tie-line, one and then another until all lines hung loosely down the side of the hull. Then I realized the welcoming gangway had already been removed. I had never been out of Denmark before. It was the first time I had even been on a boat. I stayed out on deck until land was out of sight, until my Denmark faded from the horizon. I went back to the wheel room where the dock men had taken my trunk but I soon realized that the sea air was better for me outside. The boat tossed about in this rocky water. After wrapping my head against the winds of the open ocean, I returned to the deck. I watched the gulls overhead until I got very bored. They were with us all the way, I think. For a while there was fog and eventually shapes in the fog expanded into a real city.

London was beyond my wildest dreams, although I was afraid to leave the dock area, or be alone unless I could see my new ship at all times. It was so big compared to the fishing vessel that I came in across the channel. I followed close behind the men as they carried my luggage over to the liner for my trip across the Atlantic. Once my trunk was aboard, I inquired about our sailing time and decided to walk along the dock area just a few feet from the ship.

It would be several hours of waiting for the ship to be loaded and then even more time for the tide to change, before we could sail. The solid land felt reassuring. I didn't go far. The sun was higher and warmer by that time so I left my cape in the new cabin. I regretted it later, when the seamen on the shore, again stopped and smiled as they watched me walk pass. I didn't like the way they looked at me. I was uncomfortable and anxious to get away from them. A family with four children was slowly walking away from the ship so I stayed fairly close to them, feeling protection just by their number. When they stopped for a warm drink, I stopped and tried to fade into the wall. The mother had noticed me walking behind and came over to offer me a cup of tea, too. I accepted and found that they, too, would be going to America on the same boat as I.

The sailing across the Atlantic was both rather frightening and fascinating. For days we saw only the sea and the sky. At times, where there was no sun, it seemed the sea and sky met and merged together. I lost my appetite for most of the trip. I wasn't sick but I just didn't feel like eating. I certainly had lots of time to think about leaving home for such a far-away place, and leaving Tise forever, and Borglum and Instrup. During the day, if it wasn't raining, I stayed out on deck in the fresh air. There must have been hundreds of people on that ship, maybe more. I'd never seen so many people and they were from everywhere, from Ireland and Scotland, some spoke languages I'd never heard before.

The shore-birds dropped away the second day out. There were a few stragglers on the third day but after that, we were too far away from land for them to fly, too far from any land. The winds were bitterly cold out on the open ocean. I wondered if the wind didn't pick up speed as it moved unhindered by the trees and farm buildings around home. When I went outside on the deck I had to wear all my warmest clothing, but my stomach was unsettled. I felt better outside so I just walked around wrapped up like a ball of wool. Sometimes I found a spot, with a break in the wind, to huddle in under the warming sun.

I was in steerage class. All the women and children slept on hammocks, three deep. The men slept in another cabin, probably the same way. It wasn't very comfortable but some said it was better than they'd had at home. And it didn't really matter. I did miss my feather beds at home, though. Many people got sick to their stomachs during the trip. Even when the weather wasn't particularly rough, the space below deck was pretty smelly and ugly. One day in a storm, for those who even felt like eating, we had to catch and hang onto our sliding plates. There were ridges at the edge of the table to keep dishes from dropping to the floor. Some of us were able to put some hard tack and cheese into our stomachs. I usually liked the smoked codfish at home but when the weather was really foul on the ship I didn't want it or any other food. I was glad I brought it though because at times, it did taste good. The ship served a lot of potato porridge. It didn't have much flavor but at least it was hot and I could add salt to it and improve the flavor a little bit.

At immigration in New York, I changed my name to Mary. It sounded more American than Johanna Marie. Klara had said when I got here I had to break with the ways of the old country and become a regular citizen when I could. After the long train ride, (two, really, since I changed trains in Chicago,) I arrived in Council Bluffs, Iowa. Both Klara and Mr. Meyers met my train, with the Meyers three oldest children. It was wonderful to hug my sister again. I was tired but so happy to be here. When it came time to break into our reunion, Mr. Meyers cleared his throat to leave the station for home, as if to say *stop the tears and lets get down to business.*

My English was not so good. Understanding and being understood was an effort, but both Mr. and Mrs. Meyers were very considerate to me. He was a tall and large man with a round middle that stretched his belt to cover. The only grain mill in town belonged to him. Always at harvest time, and in those first few years, he rarely came home except on Sundays. He slept at the mill. Mrs. Meyers was a large boned woman, but with not much meat on her. She looking like she bore the nine children in her flock. She does need some help, I thought.

"Mothers of nine children are always patient but efficient. If they're not, they'd lose their minds," Mrs. Meyers laughed.

For my year's labor in exchange for my fare from Denmark, I was to do all the ironing and most of the washing. The older girls helped me when they were home, but the starched petticoats they used for Sundays and all the men's shirts had to be ironed with the flat iron heated on the kitchen stove. I already knew to shake out as many wrinkles I could before hanging the clothes on the line to dry. The three older girls and I made a game as we were doing laundry. We raced to hang out or take down the most clothes from the clothes' lines.

My day started at five o'clock. I had the two cows to feed, milk, and put out to pasture. The children needed to be awakened on school days. When Mr. Meyers was home, he started the fire in the kitchen stove but on the days he stayed at the mill, I did that chore before I milked so when I came back into the house, Mrs. Meyers was up and fixing breakfast.

I worked hard, but I had always worked hard on our farm in Tise. I loved being with the children, smaller children than Mama's and Papa's families. We made things together, cookies and biscuits, made in different ways, a favorite shape for the day perhaps. At Thanksgiving time, (my first as we didn't have a Thanksgiving Day in Denmark) all of us tried to out-do the other in designing the most wicked and ghoulish of pumpkins. The Meyers' children loved to correct my English. We even made a game out of it, and I improved a lot. They called me "the Danish dunce." I didn't mind. It was all in fun.

After the year of my contract passed, Mr. Meyers offered me a salary of $19.00 a month, plus room and board, if I'd stay. I did stay. I stayed for six years.

Council Bluffs had many Danish immigrants. Klara introduced me to almost everyone she knew. On Sundays, my only day off, they all gathered in the park after church services during the good weather. It was there that I first saw Peter Christensen, several years after I first arrived. There were always young men there and we became good friends but when I first saw Peter, I felt he was special. He was taller than I, with brown hair and gray-green eyes of the palest color ever. They were almost hypnotic and he was very good looking. I saw him as he played ball with the men. Once he hit a home-run and ran gracefully for the three bases and then as he approached home-base he finished off with four hand-springs.

I didn't really meet him. We weren't introduced but we were in a group of other people and so it wasn't a very personal meeting. But, one day when I was in the carriage with Mrs. Meyers and the two younger children, I commented about little Brigit's cough. At the time we were just approaching the four corners store, so Mrs. Meyer had us stop so I could get some camphor for Brigit.

The weather had turned cold about the third week of October and our season of colds had started. Once inside the store, I circled the pot-bellied stove in the center of the room, walking directly to the rear counter where I could see the bottles of patented medicines. Apparently the clerk hadn't heard me come in so I spoke first.

"I'd like a large bottle of Camphor, please."

The clerk wheeled around at the sound of my voice. "A-ha, I didn't hear you come in."

It was Peter Christenson.

We stood counter-distance apart and I, for the first time, could stare directly into those eyes. He smiled just slightly. I took a deep breath and looked down. "I need a bottle of Camphor. "Oh yes, so you said. But you don't sound or look like you're ill," he said. "Oh no. It's not for me. It's for the child of my employer. Her cough is worse and her mother wants the Camphor."

"Of course, I have Camphor, but if I could see her, I might suggest something else, something better." Peter was almost apologetic.

"She's just outside, in the carriage."

"Well, let's go take a look." He was already on his way to the door.

Brigit was sitting on her mother's lap, red cheeked and looking feverish. She was limp and very quiet. Peter picked up her hand and spoke ever so softly to her in such a gentle and tender way that was just right for children. He asked her if the old-gray fox had gotten her? She smiled only slightly at Peter. He listened to her heavy breathing and her hoarse voice.

"Her chest is pretty congested," he said, looking straight at Mrs. Meyers. "I'd recommend something to loosen that chest. Are you familiar with Mustard plaster?"

Mrs. Meyers had never used it. She said she'd heard of it, so Peter explained the directions. "Let her sleep close to the stove tonight, with a pot of water slowly steaming all night. Continue the aspirin as usual."

Backing away, he continued. "You'll notice a difference in her breathing by morning. Take the Camphor, also. It'll help with her cough."

I followed him back into the store, but he held the door open so I could go in first. He seemed taller than when I first saw him. And he was right about Brigit. The next day she was dramatically better. Her breathing was easier and the pitch of her voice was less throaty than the day before. I had slept in the room with Brigit so I could be alert to any disruption in her sleep.

"She's better?" Mrs. Meyers asked, as she came into the room.

"Yes, just in the last hour or so. She's had fever during the night but it appears to be gone now. I'll continue with the aspirin and the cough medicine. Tonight we'll decide if we need to apply another mustard plaster."

Mrs. Meyers agreed and then mentioned the effectiveness of the mustard plaster and how surprised she was that she hadn't know about it before.

"I must stop by that store to thank the young man for his suggestion. I don't know him. Wilhelm usually shops for me but I have seen him on occasion. Do you know anything about him?"

I just smiled and shook my head. I wanted to know more about him. I hoped I would get to know him better.

And I did.

CHAPTER THREE

The Birth

New Year's eve was almost always white in Council Bluffs, and it was in this year of 1892. I leaned forward to see the sky to the North through the window above the kitchen sink. "This is wicked," I thought. It worried me. My time was near. It wasn't just the pressure on my bladder and the tight stomach, but the back pain down low where my labor pains have always been. The skin across my belly seemed weaker, thinner than before. I smiled to myself as I questioned why I shouldn't be weaker. After six pregnancies in the thirteen years of my marriage to Peter Christensen, logically my muscles would really be stretched.

I leaned to stretch over a little farther in order see the sky through the bare limbs of the great locust tree in the side yard. The twist pinched out the air from my lungs. I jerked back into a straight and upright position and struggled for a good deep breath. I stretched up to my full height, filling my lungs with as much air as my crowded body would allow, what with that boxer in there, punching and poking at me.

"Oh dear, what about this weather?" I thought out loud. Doc Lindgren is getting along in years and his rheumatism always slows him down in bad weather. It'll be hard on him to come out on a night like this, I thought. Lindgren delivered all my babies. All, that is, except that first one. That was before I knew of old Doc Lindgren. A midwife helped for that birth, a little girl. Actually, she was stillborn. Then, there was Anna, now ten.

Paul was born two years later. When he was only three, he stepped on a nail out behind the barn. He had slipped out of his sandals so he was bare footed. The nail only grazed the side of his foot, but the skin was punctured. That was all it took. He died a very painful death. It was Lockjaw. For Peter and me, it was wrenching to lose our son. Part of us died with him. He was only three and he suffered through such pain. Doc Lindgren was with him, stayed through most of the night, down to his last breath. He couldn't have been kinder if Paul had been his own child. Doc Lindgren did everything he could for him.

Esther and Inger were born next, in that order. I felt like I was always pregnant, always out of energy. It seems that I'm always pregnant. I love my girls but I wish . . .

"Mama. Mama. Can't you hear me?"

Three year old Inger was sitting at the kitchen table waiting for my cookies to finish baking. I believe the smell of cinnamon and nutmeg just reached the sleeping loft because here come the footsteps, slapping and clanking on the wood of the stairs. "There always seems to be that urgency in food, particularly in a warm, winter house." I smiled to myself.

"I'm sorry, dear. What did you say?" I turned to face Inger.

"How much longer? I'm hungry. I want some pfefferneuse," she said, just as her older sisters bounced into the room.

"That's why we're here, and not a moment too soon," Anna panted.

"I think they're about ready," I said as I opened the oven above the firebox of the old iron cook stove. Yes, they are a fine brown color, toastie and rich, not too dark and not too light. Not a minute too soon," I repeated.

"The pan is hot. Don't touch!" I was loud and clear as I pulled them from the oven and set the metal sheet on two iron trivets in the center of the long wooden kitchen table.

"Pfepperneuse in the wintertime is like fresh air in the springtime; their spicy flavors curl into every corner of this old house. And I never have to call you girls down, do I? Your noses lead you in. I don't have to tie a string to your noses to bring you into the kitchen at baking time, do I?" I laughed. "Only when there's work to be done." Anna and Esther were already on their way out of the kitchen with a full basket of those tiny brown balls when the next tin of batter went into the oven to bake. I gave Inger just a little more milk as my mind drifted back to my own thoughts.

I stretch out and shrink in, deliver another baby and my tummy flattens somewhat. Just like the air in the bag-pipes. But then that's not my skin and muscles. It seems that each time after the delivery, I don't flatten like before the pregnancy. I am always pregnant, or at least, it does seem I am. I smiled to myself.

"What are you laughing at, Mama?" Inger asked.

"I'm just happy, dear? You're going to have a new sister or brother soon. Will you like that?"

I didn't listen to the answer. Maybe my time has come, maybe it'll be today. But what a day! I opened the fire box and dropped in another bunch of branches, good and dry, to bring up a full, hot fire quickly. A small log went in next. I could see my youngest out of the side of my eye. Apparently after having stuffed herself with the tiny cookie balls, she was now rolling them across the table in her own game.

"Inger, pfefferneuse are not for." I turned with a twist, from the stove to the table and felt a 'pop' down low in my stomach and then the rush of warm fluid down the inside of both my legs.

"OH, oh, oh!" I gasped. Quietly, almost mumbling, I said, "There goes my water." I stepped back to look at the floor where I had been standing.

Inger looked down, too, pointing and started to giggle. "Mama, you puddled."

I recovered and began to lighten up, too. "You're right. I puddled. That means our new baby will be here soon. I'll need some help. Quickly go find Anna and tell her to come to the kitchen in a hurry." Inger jumped down from the bench and scampered from the room.

My lower back was a long, steady pain. At times, a deep rolling wave, more severe than others, gripped my lower torso. That was labor, I knew.

When Anna came into the kitchen, I sent her to Mrs. Brunn's house diagonally across the road. "Tell her to come as soon as possible. She'll understand." We'd already talked of this time. Word needed to be sent to Peter at the store, so he could go for Doc Lindgren.

I was an old hand at having babies. Inger started in to get my night gown, as I removed my wet bloomers and cotton stockings in the now solitude of my kitchen. There was plenty of time to clean up myself and the floor of the fluid. I was standing in my night gown, emptying the clean water from the bucket on the back porch into two large pans just as the fat Mrs. Brunn rushed in, swishing her long, black skirt behind her.

"Stop that this minute," she scolded. "Let me do that. You get in bed. Go on, get out of here, into your bed. Shu, shu," she spoke as though she was clearing a path through her chicken pen. She was stern and cross, as she set the pans on the stove to heat.

Outside, the storm had turned into a hard blowing, chill biting animal. It as fierce. The wind whistled in long streams of gasping air. The snow fell in great, thick flurries that produced a gray air, looking almost like fog. Behind those sheets, the darkening sky saluted the approaching night. Mrs. Brunn left to send her seventeen year old son, Heinrich, to Peter's store with the important message.

Peter later told me that almost every customer coming into the store that day had spoken of the weather. Each person had tarried a few minutes to warm themselves over the potbellied stove in the center of the building, before heading back out into the cold again. An hour earlier, Peter had looked across the road to the blacksmith shop. He glanced out again. Now it wasn't there. Oh, it was there all right. There was a dim glow of the working fire through the haze of falling snow and frosty air, but the building was completely hidden by the storm.

When Heinrich Brunn came through the front door, Peter was high on the ladder, stacking large flower printed bags of flour on the upper shelves. He quickly slipped down the ladder as Heinrich explained his mission. "I'm on my way to see a pretty lady about a baby, a new one," he yelled to his brother in the back of the store."

He buttoned his coat as he left the warm room and glided down the outside steps. Walking out to the small stable that housed the horses, the soft powdery snow told him he must change his plan. He saddled his horse, knowing that traveling without the buggy gave him more speed and flexibility. Peter rode for 30 or 40 minutes toward the bridge over the river. It was usually a 15 minute ride on horseback, at most. Peter became very concerned. Getting to the river on the way to Doc Lindgren's is getting harder by the minute. Crossing that bridge without a railing on its side would be very hazardous without better visibility. Even if he walked his horse across, following that road to the Lindgren house might be impossible, given the change in the terrain since all the tree felling last fall. Would he be able to find his way? There were not many farms where he could get his bearings or to stop by for directions. The density of the snowfall reduced visibility to only a few feet.

"What to do now? What should I do? Could Mary do with only a midwife? Peter thought.

He later told me, he pondered on our first baby, delivered by a midwife. He felt the midwife was partially to blame for the infant's death. "Maybe she did nothing wrong," he once said. "But the point was, she also didn't do the RIGHT thing." That was it. It was a difficult delivery, being the first child and then to be breached, too. The baby simply took too long to be born. But I just didn't want to have her around me. Why should I take a chance? was my attitude.

There was another new doctor in the area but I didn't like him at all. Peter knew I didn't like him and wouldn't want to use him again. As a matter of fact, when Doc Lindgren was down with the flu last winter, I just stayed with my own fever rather than call Doctor Stevens. But, by this time, Peter figured he only had two choices. It was either the mid wife or Doctor Stevens, both unacceptable options, but he had to take the lesser of the two. He rationalized that at least Doctor Stevens had the proper schooling. He had a certificate. Peter made a choice. Doctor Stevens, it was.

It was already well past eleven o'clock when the doctor and Peter finally got though the snowdrifts and reached the turn into our house. They both dismounted just in front of the barn and Peter opened the barn door leading his horse inside. Doctor Stevens followed with his horse. Peter lifted the lantern, picked up a blanket and tossed it to the Doctor and quickly, covered his own mount with another.

When Peter and the doctor came in, I was hardly aware of them. I was wretched, so tired and wallowing in my bed wet with perspiration. I didn't even open my eyes. My pains were almost uninterrupted now. I knew Peter was there when he came over to the bed and picked up my hand.

"We're here, Lillimor." He called me that at very special times, when he was being especially tender. "The doctor and I are here with you."

I didn't see or hear the doctor. I presumed it was Doc Lindgren. I expected Doc Lindgren but I didn't ask. The pain was steady now, very hard. I pushed with all the energy I had left.

Mrs. Brunn said, "You've come not a minute too soon. The time is here."

Peter left the room, but it wasn't until the doctor told him to leave that Peter noticed the spirits on his breath. Nothing was noticeable on the outside. Here, inside the closed, warm house, he picked up the odor of alcohol. Doctor Stevens had turned away from Peter as he removed his coat. Mrs. Brunn told me later, that she saw the doctor take a gulp from a flask inside his coat, then he quickly recapped it and returned it to his pocket.

As Peter moved over to the glowing fire, he said he thought about that odor. How much alcohol had he had? Did it effect his judgment? He said later my scream interrupted his thoughts. He could hear the doctor and Mrs. Brunn talking but was not sure of what they were saying. It was just past midnight.

"That's fine, Dearie. It's a girl. A beautiful, little girl," squeaked out Doctor Stevens.

As I concentrated on my body's demands I had a hazy, very temporary thought about that voice. For the first time, I heard a voice that I didn't recognize, but it was familiar. Where had I heard it before? I knew it wasn't Doc Lindgren. But who? I felt spent, the energy rung from my body as the perspiration soaked into the quilts beneath me. I was so relieved it was over. I guess I just drifted in and out of a dream like state.

So it was another daughter. Peter had so wanted a son this time. This would make the fourth girl. We had picked out the name in advance, just in case. It was Ruth Catherine Christensen. So, Ruth, it was.

Through the exhaustion, I could hear a robust crying. There were times that I was aware the doctor was working on me. I think Mrs. Brunn was with the baby because I was aware of a slurping sound, the suction bulb used for extracting the fluid from the baby's nose and ears, over by the dresser. Usually, Mrs. Brunn's voice was robust and stern but now she talked to the baby in such a gentle and quiet voice, softened close to a whisper. Peter smiled at this usually demanding and strong woman, now so gentle. She was getting the ties ready for the umbilical cord when the doctor took over.

Doctor Stevens then tied the knot in the baby 's cord with a double circle, clipping the string ends and putting the now more agitated infant onto her back. Mrs. Brunn said he checked the two nostrils for fluid causing her to remind him that she had already done that.

"Oh, so ya said." He turned to his bag and after a search removed the bottle of silver nitrate that he had mixed just yesterday.

Without hesitation, Doctor Stevens removed the bottle, opened it, and squeezed the black bulb to fill the dropper with the solution, giving no thought about which solution he had picked up. The hour was late and the room quite warm. He was hurrying to finish what he had to do and return to his own home.

He opened the baby's left eye and squeezed something in the small bulb of the dropper into her eye. He repeated the process on the other eye. He paid no attention to the little jerk in the baby's body as the first solution hit her eyes. She was already screaming. This was a beautiful, normal child, it appeared. Peter had been summoned by Mrs. Brunn and was watching this process from his wife's bedside.

With the eye cleaning completed, he handed the baby to Mrs. Brunn who promptly began to diaper and dress the crying infant. He then put on his coat and said his 'good-byes' to Peter and Mrs. Brunn, and said "Good job, Dearie," to me as he left the house.

This baby cried at lot, it seemed, more than any of the others. When the baby was dressed she was given to me, the lids of her eyes already appeared were red, redder than usual. Peter noticed it, too, but he said nothing as Doctor Stevens was already out the door. It was only the following day that Peter noticed the swelling of the lids. He said nothing to me, thinking he would save me any unnecessary worry, but unknown to me, he went for the doctor.

Peter got no answer to the knock on Dr. Stevens office door. Peter went back to the store and tried again later in the day. He still wasn't in so Peter rode out to his house. A thin and homely woman answered the door and identified herself as the doctor's wife. She said the doctor was out on a house call. Peter told Mrs. Stevens of his observations and asked that the doctor come out as soon as he returned. She agreed and Peter left her porch.

However, as he turned his horse to leave the Stevens' yard, Peter noticed the barn to the right rear of the house with the barn door slightly ajar. The horse that Doctor Stevens had ridden on New Year's Eve was inside the barn. The buggy was inside, also. Maybe, he had more than one horse. Perhaps he took a different horse, he speculated as he headed back home.

By the end of the next day, there was discharge from the baby's eyes. Peter tried, ever so gently, to open her eyes. The lids couldn't be separated. They were crusty and stuck together. Then, he had to talk to me about it.

We had to get the doctor back to see Ruth and apparently he wasn't coming. Peter had brought home a bottle of Boric Acid from the store. He held it close to the stove to remove the chill from the solution and then dabbed the cotton filled solution at Ruth's eyes. I held her while he struggled with the still swollen eyes. By removing the dried crust from her eyelids, we felt we could see the eyes themselves. We still couldn't open her eyes.

I was frightened as I watched him. "What's wrong, Peter? What is it?"

He studied her eyes a minute before answering the question? "There are white flakes in the discharge. I don't think this is an infection." He turned to look at me.

"Then, what? What could it be?" I asked.

I knew he was afraid, but he couldn't deal with my fear, too. "I don't know. But its time we found out."

Determined to get Doctor Stevens back to see our baby, Peter left early the next morning and went directly to his home. Again he reported, Mrs. Stevens answered the door and refused to "wake up" her husband. Again, Peter explained the problem and insisted on talking to the doctor, directly. He became more insistent, raising the level of his voice to Mrs. Stevens until another door opened up a little way down the hall. Doctor Stevens emerged, dressed, not in his night clothes, but shoeless and in a very rumpled suit. He was very unsteady on his feet.

Just inside the entrance, face to face with Doctor Stevens, Peter could see the excessive dilation of his pupils. His nostrils detected a foul breath of stale alcohol. Peter realized that the doctor had been drinking. He wondered about his condition on New Year's Eve. Why hadn't he known that Stevens was unreliable? Why had he not known about a drinking problem?

Peter's anger began to build as he struggled to control himself. "My new baby's eyes are swollen and red. There's white discharge and crusted matter of the sides."

Doctor Sevens interrupted. "sa probably an insection and . . ."

This time Peter did the interrupting, his voice level raising. "No infection, Dr. Stevens. It's not possible. Mrs. Brunn saw you clean her eyes."

Ignoring Peter's confrontation, Dr. Stevens continued. "Ya might want to use some boris asad and I'd say," he hesitated to take aim at another recommendation. He continued. "Give 'em a good washin', a, a coupla times a day, I say."

Peter realized this doctor was worse than incompetent. He was dangerous. Probably he didn't even know what he was doing when he came over New Year's Eve. Certainly he shouldn't come close to our baby, now. He can't be trusted. Peter made a mental note of the pupil dilation in the bright morning light. He would find out what it meant at a later time.

Peter wheeled around and ran to his horse, struggling to control his anger. He jumped on and turned toward the river bridge. An hour later he was riding up to our house in Doc Lindgren's buggy, with his own horse trailing behind. Peter helped the elderly doctor down. Although the day was sunny and clear, the doctor noted aloud that the effects of the cold caused him pain. Doc Lindgren's back stooped as he walked. He examined our restless baby from head to toe, cooing and coddling as he exuded his warmth and tenderness. He wrapped Ruth in her blanket and set her back into my arms. He quieted and became pensive. He then cut through the chaff.

"This situation is not new to me. I've seen it more times than I'd like to recall. We'll have to wait a couple weeks for those eyes to heal so we can see in. There's nothing we can do now."

Peter reached for my hand.

"Apply cold compresses at least once every hour and sponge off the discharge with the boric acid, as needed."

Peter explained, "I've been loosening the discharge of her eyes with the boric acid, already."

"Good. That's good. Keep it up," he paused. Then quietly, he added. "Two cents worth of boric acid would have prevented this." He narrowed his lips and slowly, shook his head back and forth.

"How bad is it?" I asked.

"Her eyes are burned. My guess is it was the silver nitrate. After the burn heals, scar tissue forms."

"How could this happen?" I asked, tense and scared.

"Probably Doctor Stevens mixed his own silver nitrate solution. We all do, you know. It's impossible to know if he just got mixed up in his proportions or if he picked up the wrong bottle from his bag. There's nothing to be done now. There's a fine doctor in Omaha, one who specializes in the eyes. When the weather breaks you'll want to take her to him. I'll take another look in two weeks, if you like, but I want you to see him, too. He wrote the name and address on a piece of paper and handed it to Peter."

When he got to the door, he turned to Peter. "The blind asylums are full today because of this kind of medicine."

Peter's mind was locked onto the words BLIND ASYLUMS. "My god, no! No! Those are crazy houses. No child of mine would be put in there. I won't allow it." His face flushed red and his neck muscles stood taut.

CHAPTER FOUR

Trip To Omaha

The name on the note from Doc Lindgren was Dr. Throckmorton P. Clay, specializing in diseases of the eye, Omaha, Nebraska. Omaha was on the other side of the river from Council Bluffs, a different state but not that far away from our home. It took some time to get to his office with the buggy ride to the ferry at the river, the ride over and the walk to Dr Clay's office. Mrs. Brunn agreed to watch the girls for what we understood to be some time before we could return home.

Many people were already in his office by the time we arrived. I'd never seen so many people in a doctor's office before. I'd never seen a whole room for waiting patients, either. Back in Council Bluffs, when another person needed to see the doctor at the same time as the doctor was seeing another patient, he waited outside. Once, when I worked for the Meyers, their doctor had chairs set up in the hall just in case another patient came in when he was busy.

Two young men who were waiting wore glasses with smoky lenses in them. Another patient, a little girl had white bandages over both eyes. I wondered if she was like our Ruth and maybe this doctor was able to fix her eyes. On one wall were a pair of oak doors with etched glass in the upper half. There were bright lights on the other side of those doors. I wondered what they were doing inside. One-by-one, these doors opened and a full skirted lady called in another waiting person or group from our midst, only to expel the same group after a short time, some smiling and others somber faced. It was a long two hours of waiting with a restless Ruth before she finally quieted into sleep. It wasn't five minutes later that the middle-aged lady in the starched, white dress came out and called out, "Christensen."

Peter took Ruth from my arms. We walked through the glass doors into the room of the bright lights. A tall, graying man wearing a white short coat was already in the room. He was leaning over a desk of many papers as we walked in. After reading for a minute, he turned around and the lady in white introduced us to Dr. Throckmorton P. Clay. She then took Ruth from Peter and laid her on the table in the center of the room.

The doctor shook Peter's hand and bowed just slightly with a gentle tilt of his head and a warm smile over his face. I liked him instantly. He seemed so kind and tender. His small goatee reminded me of my own Papa back home in Denmark.

"I've read the letter you brought from your family doctor, Doctor Lindgren, isn't it?" Peter nodded and he continued, "Well, let's see what we have here," and turned to a now squirming infant.

"Well, aren't you a beauty?" he said, setting his little finger into the palm of her curled up hand. Speaking just a few inches from her face, in almost a whisper, as if the conversation was only between him and Ruth, he said.

"We're not so nice here, taking you away from your warm spot there on papa's shoulder. But we'll be friends and I'll let you go back in just a minute." His well-coordinated assistant efficiently moved right in as if she could read his mind. She handed him a small electric light in a metal tub, and then took hold of one of Ruth's arms with one hand and her head with the other. Dr Clay's right hand held the light as he spread open the eye with the forefinger and thumb of his left hand.

He began a soft hum as he bent over our baby, staring intently through the separated eye lids. He was only a few inches above her face. He stopped his hum for only a split second. For such a long time, he stared into her eye. Then he moved to the left eye. After a very short time with that eye, he stopped. His assistant said nothing until Ruth began to squirm. She then leaned forward, also and Dr. Clay spoke very quietly to her, too quiet for me to hear.

I searched his face for a clue. "Please, God, let him have good news for us." But his brow furrowed, ever so slightly. One of his hands pulled off the head band with the mirrored lens from his head as the other hand replaced his eye-glasses on his nose. He scooped up our baby, talking to her as he turned to hand her to Peter.

"Now, that wasn't so bad, was it?" His eyes were sad eyes, but the outer edges of his lips softened into grandfatherly warmth and understanding. He avoided looking directly at either Peter or me. He took a deep breath and settled against the examining table, taking his time to empty all the air from his lungs.

I was hopeful when he was relaxed enough to hum. But then the hesitancy meant something. What was it?

"You must realize the seriousness of your child's eyes. They are pretty well healed from the initial injury but . . ."

Right away, I stammered, "But what can you do to reverse it, to make it better?"

"I'm so sorry. The damage has been done. There's nothing to be done now, by me or anyone else."

I swallowed hard, having just heard the expert speak, not wanting to hear him, resisting the meaning of his words. I guess I really knew it almost from the beginning. I looked over at Peter and could sense his pain. He was stiff and taut. His eyes were moist and he stood looking out the window, staring but not seeing. My seeing Ruth in his arms, I began to hear the words again, those dreaded words spoken a few short minutes before.

"How could this happen? Why did it happen?" I pleaded.

"While still in the womb, infants are exposed to bacteria from the mother's body. Upon delivery, and exposure to the outside air those bacteria will grow and infections can set in. This is a particular problem with the eyes. Both the ears and the nose are a little different. Of course we expect them to be well cleaned at birth along with the rest of the child's body. With the depth of space under the eye-lids germs are harder to get at. Particularly in view of the fact that the lachrymal gland continually secrets fluid to keep the eye moist. The membrane of the eyeballs are fragile and very tender, so we are limited in what we can use to kill the bacteria and not damage the eyes.

"Have you ever heard of Baby Sore Eyes?" he asked. "Another term for it is Cold in the Eyes. We doctors refer to it as Ophthalmia Neonatorum. It's one of the most common forms of unnecessary blindness. All doctors are concerned about this problem. As a matter of fact, so are many young mothers, but they don't understand it. Sometimes they resist eye washing for fear of eye damage. But the fact is, much blindness is caused by infections because the eyes are NOT properly cleaned at birth.

One-half of all blindness in this country is preventable. The longer the delay in getting good medical care, the more serious the result. And once the problem commences the loss of at least some sight is highly probable. Our job is to catch the problem early. Even a few drops of a simple medicine in the baby's eyes prevent the problem in almost all cases. At least that plan is appropriate if we're only speaking of infection.

Many years ago a great doctor in Germany found that if he put a mild medicine into the eyes as soon as the baby is born, the disease is prevented in almost all cases. Nurses and mid wives use this more and more now. It does make the baby's eyes red and sore for a day or two, and mothers and friends think the result is the cause of the medicine and refuse to use it. The fact is the use of the medicine will prevent the disease that is so dangerous.

"Other parents think the red eyes are the result of some shameful disease of the parents. Parents have nothing to do with this problem. They aren't to blame. But they always want their babies to be perfect and often can't face the suggestion of a problem.

"The simple medicine the German doctor used was a light solution of silver nitrate. We've long used a 10% solution of silver nitrate to cauterize wounds but for eye cleansing we use a ratio of 1%. Every doctor carries a supply of both proportions in his black bag. It is Federal law that this eye cleansing be done with every birth. I have no question that this was used on your daughter." He looked at Peter and then at me, alternately back at Peter and then me, as if searching for an expression to expose our states of mind.

"Most of us mix our own solution. It's my educated guess that the wrong solution or the incorrect ratio was used on her eyes resulting in burning the eyes. Your doctor may have inadvertently picked up the wrong bottle from his bag. Perhaps the bottle wasn't shaken to mix so his dropper picked up the stronger silver nitrate, which settled at the bottom. That doesn't matter at this point." He flipped his hand in the air and shifted his weight to the other foot.

He continued, "Both of Ruth's eyes are substantially damaged. The scarring creates a white covering that is pretty generalized over both eyes."

Both Peter and I were transfixed and hung to every word. He continued.

"It is possible that she may be able to see a little light which would certainly give her some advantage. Also, perhaps some colors. I wouldn't expect much. But the true test will have to be when Ruth grows enough to tell us how much she can see through those scars. Don't get your hopes up. If she can see anything it would be minor. Looking at the bright side of this unfortunate accident, you are indeed in the best place to deal with this child. We're almost in the 20th century now. And you're living in the most progressive country about those in our society with handicaps. Old attitudes about blindness have changed a great deal over this past century, both here and abroad. Around the world various societies have changed the life of the blind from that of begging on the street or being put into prisons and treated like mentally unbalanced persons, to giving them training and education. We want them to be able to earn a living, to be independent. There are many occupations they are well suited for. It's important that you remember her limitation only effects her eyes. That is at this time we have no reason to think otherwise. Judging from your families' histories, I have no reason to believe she won't be otherwise perfect.

Peter and I had listened intently to all he had to say. He stood up, straightening his back and said. "Any more questions?" After a pause, "Let me know if I can be of any help."

Both of us had searched his words and his face for anything that he had to say to give us encouragement, hoping for something to try, for some chance operation. We heard no good news and we knew our time with him was over. We needed to leave. Peter shook Dr. Clay's hand. "Thank you, sir. I much appreciate your time."

As we waited for the ferry to return us to Council Bluffs, I removed some of the food from the basket I brought with us. I unwrapped a broken hunk of oatmeal bread, baked just yesterday. I broke off a piece and handed it to Peter. The cheese had been sliced at home so I just set the napkins of our dinner between us. Not much was said as we ate. I was just finishing chewing a dried apple slice when Ruth began to stir. I drew her close to me.

On the buggy ride from town to our house I had much to think about. I watched the snow-covered fields and roof tops pass before me as my baby nursed. My body was tired and my mind traveled as the buggy moved. The rhythm in the "clop-clop" of the horse's hooves was good to hear but I would have preferred not to have that occasional gift of dirty snow thrown into my lap from their hooves. That occasional distraction was good as I watched Ruth as she slept, my damaged child. I had not protected her. I had not been able to correct the injury. My mind moved far away, back to our home in Council Bluffs and I tensed as I thought of the night of delivery, of that doctor. Ruth's tiny body felt warm against mine, alive and otherwise healthy, or so said Dr. Throckmorton P. Clay. Peter had tucked us in well for the ride back to the house. The winter sun had dropped on the horizon displaying a near full moon. It illuminated the blanket of snow and created dancing shadows as we crossed the countryside. Smoke trailed out from the top of chimneys and occasionally a spray of bright embers showered the night sky. The lighted windows of the farm houses gave me company as I visualized the families sitting around the stove in the center of the house or maybe they sat together around the table playing cards. I yearned to be back with my little family. It had been a long day. I was so tired.

Mrs. Brunn had fed the girls and brought them home. There was a fine fire warming the house as we arrived home. Just before I climbed into bed, I got down on my knees. "Help me, Lord. Show me what I must do for Ruth. Guide me and give me Your wisdom, for I need You now more than I ever have. Be with this family, help us all, look over us and give us your blessed guidance. Amen."

CHAPTER FIVE

Infant Days

In the first months after birth, it seemed that caring for Ruth was no different than raising any of the other children. All summer long I watched for an effort to crawl from her. She did not crawl. As I look back on it, I'm not even sure she squirmed and wiggled like the others. It didn't occur to me that her eyes had any relation to her physical development. By the fall, I had begun to wonder if she was really very bright. The other children smiled earlier, all of them. Ruth didn't smile. I began to think about that a lot. It was depressing to me. My God, it was a devastating thought. Was it possible that I didn't just have a blind child but also a dull one? Although, on one occasion I noticed when Inger came in to talk with her, she flayed her arms and stretched her little legs into jerky excitement. This surprised me.

One evening after Peter had finished bringing in the firewood for the next day's cooking, I sat down to nurse Ruth. The girls had gone over to the Brunn's, at her son Heinrich's, urging. One of their horses was old, gentle enough for the children to ride and so Mrs. Brunn had agreed to this time after supper. I was aware that Peter was very quiet. He had been that way all evening. Now that I think about it, he seemed to be quietly observing both his new daughter and me for some time, now.

He often had his quiet times, when he talked little and thought a lot. Other times, if the children were close by, he laughed and played light games with them. At these times, he was much more outward. In those quiet times he played games of cards or marbles, or he told them stories. In the summer, it was hide and seek, pyramid building and yarn-spinning outside on the grass.

His stories were of the old home-place in Denmark. There was the story of Bertha, the pet cow of his childhood who wouldn't let strangers near her but Peter thought Bertha communicated with him through her eyes. Or when his mama cat disappeared, his mama dog let the cat's babies nurse her. His humor was light for his tendency to exaggerate was irrepressible. He seemed to be almost clairvoyant for he had such fine powers in the observation of people. He knew almost before they did, of a coming fever or cold. He could tell when they were distressed, no matter how well they tried to hide it. He always seemed to know. His perception was greater than a man twice his age.

"My darling, Lillemor," Peter started, "you've been so busy with the children, so pre-occupied and afraid of what problems we might have with Ruth, that many opportunities are passing us by."

I couldn't accept a single criticism from him, particularly now. I stopped rocking. Anger boiled up inside me and I started to speak. He cut me off, again, in his gentle and calm voice.

"I see the grief in your eyes. You've been slower to recover from this birth than with any of our other children. You seem overwhelmed by the enormity of her problem, our problem. You've always been such a loving mother, but you are awkward with Ruth. I've noticed you don't talk to her as you did the others. You are allowing your sadness to effect your attitude not only of Ruth but of the other children."

"Now, just a minute." I stopped him this time. My voice cracked in emotion, "You don't seem to realize the work to be done here. And I'm tired all the time."

Peter sat quietly, his green eyes searching my face as I exploded with my deepest thoughts. I continued. "I can't seem to get my strength back this time after having this baby. All our girls are good little helpers, I can't complain about that but . . ."

Peter broke in. "I know that, my dear. You're so little and now you look frail and tired all the time. I am concerned about all the demands of the children and the house. I worry about your health!

"Are you worried about Ruth, about her crawling?" He didn't wait for me to answer when he continued. "But consider this. She can't see objects around her. Ruth has no incentive to reach out. There's no reason to stretch because she doesn't know anything is there. She doesn't even try to move very much. Her learning process is different. The way I see it, learning can't take place as it should, as it did with our other children. I think she sees light because I've noticed how she usually turns her head toward the window or the burning glow in the open stove. She doesn't see enough to respond with her hands, although she seems to try to raise up when there is sunlight coming through the window."

I watched him rise from his chair and pace the room as if searching through his thoughts.

"She doesn't see. Well, she does see some, not enough to respond with her hands, not enough to have an example to follow. Her curiosity is missing since she's unable to follow objects and people around and curiosity is what entices all of us to investigate. From that, we learn."

"Right now, we're the problem, Mary. Not Ruth. And soon, the older children will have more problems. They feel the impact of a new baby and your time away from them to be with the new one. Most of all they're very perceptive to our moods and begin to feel our emotions."

I took a deep breath. I tried to relax. He did say "we're the problem." I just let him talk.

"Children have lots of bounce. The older ones are tough and have the ability to take much of the load off you, both emotionally and physically, without hurting themselves. In fact, they actually mature better with having many more of the responsibilities that you have, with being and feeling part of the family. You and I must set the example, the example in caring and loving, in sharing and in being needed."

Ruth was stretched over my shoulder. I got up and left the room without saying a word. In our bedroom, I laid her in her cradle, took the hem of my long skirt and wiped my face. I walked back into the main room. Peter was standing by the window, responding to the sounds of his daughters coming from the house across the road.

"Oh Peter, I'm so ashamed. I've lost much of my pride and self confidence. This problem is almost more than I can bear. I'm really very proud of my family, of my girls but for such a long time, I've been so tired." I paused for several seconds.

"This ugly depression has taken its toll on me. I know I can't continue like this." I paused to keep from bursting. I took a deep breath and then dropped my head down into my hands and just waited for time.

Peter spoke softly. "I have a plan. Are you ready to listen to it?" He was forcing me to concentrate on his words, as he walked back to face me. I nodded and blew my nose with a handkerchief. I returned to my rocking chair and slowly rolled back and forth, as he spoke.

"Believe in your heart that Ruth is normal. Know that she sees, thinks and hears like all the other chil . . ."

"Peter," I called out crossly. "How can I know that? She doesn't see. She doesn't think, or maybe she doesn't even hear us normally."

"You don't know that. That is, you don't know how much she sees and you don't know anything else for sure. You only are suspicious about it. That's not the right approach to the problem. You must get a hold of yourself and accept the situation we have, whatever that is."

My lips trembled as I watched him speak. He continued.

"Just relax. We have to do the best we can with and for her. Keep your mind open about her and believe in her. Believe she can do everything our other children can do. Every time you nurse, or hold her, speak ever so softly to her. Tell her of your hopes and dreams, hopes and dreams for her, for the other girls and for our family. Make her your best friend. Tell her how lucky we are to have come to America."

"Peter, you're out of your mind. She can't understand."

"No, I'm not," he interrupted. Listen to me. Let the other children hear you, too. Wipe out all the fears from your mind, the anger and depression. If you don't, they'll grow and fester. They'll spread poison and will make you sick. Pick yourself up and you can take yourself out of your sadness. You are responsible for your own attitude and you can make it different. You can make it better."

I knew he was right. He always was about these things. I had given him my attention and now, it was my turn to speak. I took advantage of it.

"I know you must be right, Peter. I'm sorry. I'll do my best."

He took his feet from the rag rug and stretched his legs for a more comfortable position as I continued. "And I want to talk with you, too. I love you and I love my children. I couldn't think of my life without you. But, I'm tired. I'm tired all the time."

I turned to meet his look straight on. "Peter, I don't want to have any more children."

Peter stiffened and his eyes widened. "I don't believe what I'm hearing. I thought you enjoyed our bed as much as I did! There must be something else?"

I quickly broke into this line with, "Nothing. Nothing, except that I cannot see any break for me but to continue having babies as long as my body holds out. But I want more for my children than more brothers and sisters to feed. I want a quality of life that we can only have if I have more time to spend with the children I have."

I knew he could understand this line of reasoning and it was truly what I felt. "I want music and dancing for them, not cleaning, cooking, and housework. I want time for picnics at the river, while you fish the stream. I want to play with them rather than grow a stomach too big to get up off the picnic blanket."

I had much to say. "You're right about doing for Ruth but all my children need me. With a blind baby, I'll have even more demands on me than ever. And she needs me more than you do, Peter."

"I wish there was another way, Lillemor. I've really tried but . . ." He got quiet again. He was silent for several minutes. "Well, since we're making big decisions now, Mary, I have something to talk to you about. I am now sure I want to study medicine. I want to be a doctor."

This did not surprise me. He'd always shown a strong interest in helping people who hurt, in helping sick people. We often talked about how natural he was in these matters.

"Peter, do you understand the time and money we'd need? And how could we live with you in school? Are you sure this is what you want?" I had a bushel basket of questions.

"Yes. I'm sure. I must. I know I'd be a very good doctor, no stupid mistakes like Doctor Stevens."

"Is Doctor Stevens the reason for your decision?" I asked.

"Not really. I believe I think like a doctor. Certainly, customers at the store will only come to me if they need a question answered about what ails them. My brother teases me about it. He calls me Brother Doc," and a pleasurable smile stretched out the corners of his mouth.

I watched him closely. I understood and believed in him. And I always have wanted the best for him. "You've had that dream for a long time, Peter. I don't know how we'll manage with your school expenses and the family." I began to ponder the full impact of such a decision.

"I don't know either, but this is very important to me. I must do everything I can do to make it work. Will you help me?" he asked.

"Of course, I will. Somehow we can work it out. I'll try. I'll do what I can."

"Let me write to some schools," Peter suggested. He continued.

"In the meantime, we have some very important matters right here. Anna is almost eleven and Esther's seven. They already help but let's look for additional ways to teach them family care and at the same time, give you time for yourself. You need time to take long walks and enjoy the spring flowers now."

The children burst into the room, all talking at once, about the "big horse that they rode on with Heinrich." "I held onto Heinrich's waist to keep from falling off," and "I wasn't even scared, either."

I left for the kitchen to fill the wash basin and bring in the towel and wash-cloth from the back porch. "Bed time, girls. Come on in for your washing." Within 10 minutes, they were tucked into their loft beds.

"Let's go to bed, too," I said.

The next morning, I got up before Peter and was writing at the kitchen table when he came in.

"So early, Lillemor? Are you writing to your mother?"

"No. I've made a list of the things we talked about last night. The things we're not going to do anymore. Do we have an empty cigar box for them?" "What for," Peter smiled and pulled an old cigar box down from the top of the cooler.

Grinning, "Now what's on you mind? I can tell by that look on your face you're into some strange ways?"

"Peter, we've going to bury all these sad thoughts and unhappy feelings. The cigar box is their casket. We'll lay them away with a kindly and proper service. They'll rest and so can we." I tossed my head back and laughed.

Peter played along, his eyes laughing as he said. "I'll get the shovel and dig a hole. Come on out when you're ready."

The maples had begun to turn to yellows and golds for the evenings were already cooler. The yard odors were not as ripe after the late night rain shower. This was the first I hadn't noticed the pigeons cooing in the eves of the barn. I felt different, lighter, when I went out with Peter. Together, we had our burial service. Peter set the box down gently into the pit, covered it with the dark and damp soil he had just removed. Picking up my hand, he closed his eyes and he lifted his face up to the sky. The outer edges of his mouth, tilted upward and his lips opened into a slight smile.

"Lord, help us put to rest all our fears and doubts.
Keep them here and don't let them out."

As he opened his eyes he spotted our family mutt, sniffing at the spot of the freshly moved earth. He added . . .

"And don't let old Corn-Cob, here, dig them up. Amen!"

We both broke up laughing and turned to hug each other.

When Peter returned home that evening, he stopped by the tiny grave and pushed a small stake into the ground. On the paper nailed to the top of the stake were the words:

Here lies D. F. Christensen
His usefulness passed
Long hold him here, at least
Or may he rest here in peace

"I don't understand the D and F Christensen?" I asked.

"Doubts and fears," he answered.

I smiled. I understood.

The tension of yesterday's conversation had been broken. This is a new day.

CHAPTER SIX

The Toddler

It was late September that I was in the back yard washing in the caldron over the open fire. The two older girls were already back in school leaving just Inger and me with the baby. For safety, I had set the boundary for children's play at the string of clothes lines separating the fire-pit from the house. As I was hanging out the laundry, I noticed Inger playing with her doll. Each morning, she either played on the front porch that wrapped the front of the house, or under the big elm tree in the back. I could hear her talking to her Christmas doll as she pushed her about in her buggy. Frequently, I had listened to her jabbering with the doll without really digesting her words. Now, in listening more intently, I realized Inger was talking to her doll just as I talked to Ruth. I stopped for a moment to listen.

Why hadn't I thought of it before? Ruth was like a doll. She was about the size of a doll. She'd fit in the doll buggy, at least she would for a while.

"Inger, how'd you like to play with your baby sister like you're playing with your doll?"

"I do, already, Mama."

"I know you do when the baby's on the bed or on the floor. You talk to her then and help her hold things. But, I mean to take her riding in your buggy and talk to her just like you talk to your doll."

"Can I bring her outside? Oh, could I, Mama? Could I?" she begged.

"Well, let's try it for a while. You must be very careful not to let the buggy tip over. The real baby will hurt easier than your baby doll. Since we're outside, I think our real baby would like to be outside, too." I reasoned.

"Play like you're a Lillemor, a little mother. You can ride your little sister all around the road to the barn, or to the edge of the pasture or almost any other place in the yard, except the well. Don't go out to the well or the road in the front of the house, but you can go all the places you have played with your older sisters. Take good care of her like Papa and I take care of you."

Inger laughed and said, "She's my baby. I'll take care of her like she was MY baby."

"You can play like you're going to Papa's store to buy some corn and potatoes for dinner."

Ruth stayed in the buggy, seemingly aware of the change in her environment. As I watched her actions on the outside, I realized that things were different on the outside of the house. She knew it. The winds were different outside. They were even different on the front porch than in the front yard. If they were strong enough to herald an impending storm, she became restless. Soft winds gently rustling the leaves above her were like lullabies. The smells of the barn animals were stronger outside, and not as strong in front of the house as in the rear. She was closer to the fresh smells of the drying cornstalks, and the sweet fragrance still left of the rose trellis at the end of the porch. The exposures to new senses were presented for her use when her development progressed to that degree.

The sounds were also different. She was closer to the sounds of the wagon wheels and the clop of horses' hoofs on the dirt road in the front of our farm home.

Ruth moved her head toward the sounds of the voices of any of the others in the family. Familiar persons brought the flailing of her little arms in excitement, but when a strange voice was heard she became still and pensive. She stiffened and cried when our neighbor, farmer Able came into the yard and started to pick her up.

Each of our girls had different personalities, of course, and each played with their youngest sister in a different way. In some ways it seemed that they treated her as if she were completely normal but in other ways, there was a subtle recollection that needed to be done differently, to encourage Ruth to feel, or smell, or hear.

Ruth was a happy baby. Bells and squeaky toys got her attention and she always became still when Inger or one of her older sisters rattled a piece of paper close to her. We included her in everything we did, except, of course, when she was sleeping or ready for sleep. She cooed with pleasure with Peter's stroking her chin or cheek. Everyone in the family would do the same, or hold her hand and cuddle her during most of her waking hours.

Peter gave her back rubs. He said "she purred like a kitten," at that time. She would get very still and her face had a look of wonderment and pleasure.

Everyone in the family talked to her as they played with her or changed her diaper. It was funny to listen to Anna tell her about her church and school. Inger, whose age was so close and was home when the others went away to school during the day, spent the most time with her. Ruth absorbed her attention like food for the hungry.

Peter's keen perception and observations were invaluable to me at this time. I was more absorbed in canning the peaches from the summer's harvest or shelling the corn to take to the mill to be ground into cornmeal, but he studied Ruth's subtle reactions. When Ruth showed no interest in crawling, Peter noticed that she stretched out on the hooked rug on the living room floor. She made no effort to move. She'd lie on her stomach, immobile for long periods of time, not even moving or lifting her head.

"She prefers to lie face down," Peter said to me one Sunday afternoon. "It must be the sensation of touch that she's aware of. Look at her. She's not asleep. She just loves the feel of the rug and the support from the sturdy floor for head and limbs. I think she senses safety there, also."

Esther had her share of chores. However, the heaviest burden fell on our oldest child, Anna, as she rather automatically became the children's leader. Anna had shown an aptitude for sewing, so during the summer, I taught her everything I knew about sewing. From that point on she made her own clothes and eventually, with my help, made our clothes, as well. She could mend and alter other clothes for her sisters, since all the children's clothing was passed on to her growing younger sisters. I helped with the hand sewing at night.

Anna was a great help for me. I relied heavily on her. And I, eventually, began to worry that Anna was too busy doing her chores for the family that she was not having a lot of fun for herself. Her favorite past-time was singing at school.

It was sometime later that one day, in the following spring that I learned at church one Sunday, about the recently widowed Mrs. Larson. I heard she would be returning to Denmark permanently. She had lost her only child to consumption and had no relatives here. She wanted to be near her family and birthplace in the "old country." I remembered she had a pump organ. Certainly she wouldn't be taking it back with her. When church was over, I went over to inquire about the organ. Indeed it was for sale, she set her price and Peter agreed it was a good buy. He picked it up in the wagon the next week and moved it into our house.

Anna was thrilled with the new acquisition. She became quite adept at pumping the bellows full of air with the foot pedals, while picking out the melodies she had sung at school and church. I taught her all I knew. But soon, she was taking lessons from the church organist. Without any prodding from me, she practiced at least an hour every day. Ruth was never very far away during this time, often moving directly up to the base of the organ.

In a little over a year, Anna began playing for the children's singing at Sunday school and she established a bit of popularity because of it. Anna wasn't a pretty girl. Even though she had her father's lovely pale green eyes, there was a too much projection in her upper front teeth that distracted from her looks. Also, she had a strong personality. She was very opinionated. I looked for ways we might soften her disposition. The organ helped make that difference.

Peter wrote to medical schools, many schools. At first, it was just for information. So many plans needed to be made after he found out the time needed for his studies and the cost to reach his goal. It actually took several years before he was able to start. He made many applications. In return, many of those applications were rejected. Although, he understood and spoke English very well, and his enunciation was quite easily understood, he did have some trouble with his reading of the English language. In addition, the vocabulary needed to become a doctor was considered inadequate by many schools. Several times he was rejected for that reason. Of course, he was disappointed but was undaunted in his determination. Rejection deterred him not in the least.

Each night, he studied at home and he took his books to work so that during his lunch-time, he could memorize new words and practice their sounds on the others in the store. He found a used medical dictionary to study and to practice spelling the difficult medical terms. He was determined that someday he would go to medical school.

Eventually, I regained my strength. And my sense of humor returned when my depression disappeared. When Ruth could sit up well enough we put her into a walker just for a change in position. Eventually, as her feet touched the floor she soon had the mobility previously lacking. Once on wheels, realizing she had the power and ability to move around, she became very active. She made up for the lost time in crawling.

As time passed, all concerns about her mental ability changed to surprise at her learning. She'd listen to voices and move toward them. If she heard sounds of the pans in the kitchen, she was drawn like a magnet to the kitchen. If Anna was playing the organ, she'd move up close to the music. "See how responsive she is to sounds." Peter explained. "And she identifies the sounds.

"The metal on metal, or the metal on wood, mean kitchen. Music means the east corner of the main room."

"Peter, I've noticed that when the sun is coming through the windows, she moves her walker to the light and points her face up towards the sun. She rolls back and forth, into the sun and back out of it. It looks as though she is testing the warmth of the sun and now she actually seeks it."

Ruth belonged to all of us and so each family member watched for a chance to teach her. Over those early years, we taught her that stoves were hot or stoves were cold, they were smooth and hard and would burn if touched when they were hot. Touching wasn't necessary to find out if it was hot. Balls were round and could be hard, and probably harder rather than soft, but if soft, they were lighter. Rubber balls felt different than yard balls and yard balls don't even roll, except on very hard dirt. Paper made no sound if it was lying still but if moved at all it made a noise like the crackling of the burning fire.

She learned that flowers from the yard were all different. Their petals were smooth like a satin undergarment. Leaves were hard and smooth but were thin, while their stems were thicker, cold, hard and straight. If it was the roses on the trellis, the branches were not so likely to be straight, but had a gentle curve, and all the roses had thorns that would hurt or could even make her finger bleed. The branches weren't hard like the stove but were hard in a different way and were flexible. They could bend. The hard stove could not bend.

The small animals about the farm were examined for size and shape, their ears (if they could be found), noses and feet. She wanted to know why the baby chicks had skin linking their toes but not the puppies or kittens, and why the kittens had a tail, why some had fur, others had feathers. A bird with a broken neck was carefully looked over by Ruth, from beak to tail feathers. She could even see the red on the cardinal in her hand and the deep blue of the jays or the yellows, grays and blacks or grays of the other birds when she could get close to them. Their voices intrigued her for their calls were all different, one bird order from another. And of course, since she touch-examined the blue jay and could see the depth of its blue and its size, she had an instant image of a blue-jay when she heard its call.

A type of communication developed between Ruth and the birds. It was a silent one. She took out bread crusts for them. At first she put the crusts on the ground and sat a few feet away, just listening. Slowly, over the months, she narrowed the distance between herself and the bread. There were times when she would talk to the birds, almost in a whisper. I'd see them from the kitchen window. I couldn't hear Ruth but I could see her mouth moving and a lone bird, stopping his eating as if listening to her. Before her fifth birthday she knew their voices, their calls and their songs.

From very early, I knew of her temper for she wanted to examine things for herself, to SEE them and to anyone who said "NO" she screamed and cried. However, she was also reasonable and accepted a good excuse for not seeing them herself, such as "that bird flies away when I try to touch him."

"You'll just have to wait until we find a dead or injured one on the ground. Then you can see it," I explained.

Other changes and surprises came about from infancy over time. One day when she was about two and said many words we heard her say. "Papa. Home. Papa. Home."

"No, Papa will be home soon, but not yet." And, I'm ashamed to say that it was a couple of weeks before I realized every time she said "Papa. Home," that he would be in the house within a couple of minutes. All the girls came racing to hug him when he came home but then he picked up Ruth and held her for a few minutes. I was usually in the kitchen finishing the dishes with the girls, when he came into the house.

One late afternoon, dinner was all in the oven so I sat resting my feet in the chair by the back door for a few minutes. Inger and Ruth had been rolling the ball in a blocked off corner. Ruth was walking by that time. I watched her stop, hesitate, then stand up and leave the activity with her sister. She then wandered over toward the door.

"Papa. Home," she said. I said nothing as I mired in my own thoughts. I remained silent for a time, and then I noticed a distant rider. Four hooves fell in almost simultaneous sets of two hitting the ground at a time, and their sounds grew louder. The pace slowed, gradually and soon turned into a walk as he approached our barn. Then I realized that Ruth knew before all of us when her father would be home.

As she could identify the distant rhythm of a thug on the hardened pad of the road she recognized those were hooves on the dirt road. Hooves meant a horse, or horses. Rarely was livestock moved down the road and never in a run as with the clippity-clop of a running horse. A single horse meant a rider or riders. If there were of sounds with wheels or creaking sounds it was either a buggy or wagon. Generally buggies and wagons didn't move as fast as a single horse. Her father's sounds were that of a single rider and so the weight of the horse on the dirt road was identifiable. We sometimes called Ruth "doorstop," because she was always at the door when her father came in from the work.

As a two year old, metal sounds and food smells attracted her into the kitchen. Peter's curiosity about her learning phases and the way it differed from his other children kindled a like interest in the rest of us in the family.

Anna came home with school songs, simple songs about the South and Virginia, or ones written by Stephen Foster. Esther also had a love of singing and her own brand of songs to sing. Even before Ruth had reached her first birthday, when the singing began at church, she became restless until placed over my mother shoulder. There she quieted. It was clear that she liked it. Peter considered it to be the chest vibrations, or the muscle tremor in my throat as I sang, that Ruth felt and liked. On the other hand, was it something else in the music that enticed her to listen?

Our family typified a family of strong, Christian, middle-class beliefs. Life centered on our family, not just within the household and also the extended family as we chose to make it. I only had the one sister in the area and Peter, the one brother, each with several children. Just as we had done in Tise when I was a child, so we did in Council Bluffs with Klara's family, Paul's family and neighbors or church friends at the park or on the river bank. At those outside events someone always had a guitar or banjo. Uncle Paul played the violin. Sometimes an Italian neighbor played the concertina with them. Sometimes we sang and sometimes we danced. It was a wonderful time for us.

As for my own little family in Council Bluffs, summer activities began when Peter got home from the store. Supper was always served on the long, narrow table on the screened porch. It was there the release of the day's heat was first felt. After the meal was over and the kitchen cleaned, we usually gathered in the front yard to get the first of the evening breezes, when there were any. At times there were wild flowers, different kinds, a range of fragrances and colors. Their leaves were different. So were the sizes and shapes of the petals. When the older girls collected them, they let their youngest sister review all these things for their textures, shapes and stamens. Sometimes I told them the ghost stories that the children liked to hear over and over again. I loved to repeat rhymes and riddles, and often adapted them to both Ruth's experiences and her limitations.

Images were a part of her sight ability, images and colors, although they were limited to the brights, like red and orange. Those had to be fairly close to her face for detection. Some images were visible to her. If the light around an object was fairly bright, she could see the general shape of the object.

I let my imagination run away in my stories of "mice, the size of baby kittens," "elephants, the size of our hen house", or a bridge longer than our barn." I thought she could understand the relative size difference.

By the time she was three, all the characters in my stories began to wear bright colors that previous listeners had never heard about. Other sounds, textures and smells were added to the story. She knew a turkey by its distinctive gobble, the geese by their calls as they flew overhead in their migration, north or south, depending on the time of the year. She identified which of our dogs was barking by the sound and the difference between baking bread and cookies by the yeast odor or lack of. Sometimes, my storytelling stopped temporarily for better explanations for Ruth. I tried to develop and enhance the characters with emotion and over-done expression. But all the senses found a new level of inclusion in my stories so she could grow from the facet of the process.

Before the evening story telling, there might be pyramid building. Peter and I both lined up together on our hands and knees. Both of the two older girls up on the next layer. Neighbor children were sometimes included. There were stacks of bodies in our pyramids at least three stories high and often four, until all came tumbling down in a chatter of giggles and laughter.

There was usually a degree of rough-housing before the evening slowed to the prone or Indian sitting position on the quilt on the ground. We told the stories as the crickets sang their songs. The fireflies came out in those summer evenings and if the sky was very dark, there were times that Ruth claimed she could see the criss-cross of lights made by the fireflies. The girls could lie on their backs and look up at the sky. Sometimes we spoke of the stars. Ruth didn't understand the stars. She said she couldn't see them.

Usually there was singing. Peter took the bass part. I usually sang alto, Anna tenor and, during the earlier years, the other girls sang the melody in unison. Eventually, the younger girls branched out into their own harmonies, often to six-part. Together they made lovely music, each participating with their individual characters, singing obligato, counter-harmonies, and sometimes in the round. Everyone sang. The singing in front of the wintertime fireplace or outside during the summer evenings was an important and wonderful part of our lives.

The seed of music was planted early. It was watered and nourished by every member of our family with a genuine love of the art. For our child, handicapped by loss of sight, it grew into a giant in her life. She needed only an ear and a voice. She had both.

One Sunday, several months after Ruth's third birthday, Anna was playing the organ in the main room while the other girls and I set the table and completed dinner. She was playing a hymn we had just sung in church, and her father was sitting close by, singing it in his beautiful bass voice, as he often did. Esther and I hummed or sang as we worked. When I called dinner, we all sat down at the table. Just as we reached for each other's hands to circle the table for the blessing, the hymn that had just been played sounded from the organ.

Anna was the only one in the house who could play the organ. She was seated at the table. Everyone else was seated, too. All, that is, except Ruth.

"Who's playing th . . ." I stopped in the middle of my question when I completed a quick head-count. I looked at Peter and he jerked his head to look at me, and almost in precision we got up from the table and rushed to the front room so we could see the organ.

There, standing in front of the organ, was Ruth. With the remaining air in the bellows of the organ, Ruth had found enough air to force the melodic line of the hymn through the reeds of the organ. We had heard her play with the organ before but this time she had the right keys to duplicate what she just heard her sister play. She had heard it at church, she listened to the family sing it in the kitchen and her father as he sat next to her older sister.

Peter picked up Ruth and hugged her.

I was stunned. "But how? It's not possible!"

Peter smiled at me and said. "But it is possible, Lillemor. God has given us a very bright little girl. A child that does not see but one who has other, very special gifts."

That event was the first display of a rare talents Ruth started to develop. The entire family loved music. Playing and singing music was a major part of most of their good times, at church, and socials, picnics in the park with the Danish community and even at home during the evenings.

After Anna's daily practice, in exchange for her youngest sister not being a pest during that time, she established a routine of inviting Ruth up to her lap and she began to teach the child how to hold her hands "like holding a ball in the palm of your hand", the use of the black, upper keys, and basic fingering. Of course, Anna had to produce the wind for the sound through the pumping of the foot pedals, but in that way Ruth learned nursery rhymes and lullabies. Sometimes Ruth played for herself to sing. In later years, she played for her sisters to sing. But very early, her memory recorded tunes and when she could get to the organ, as long as she had someone to pump the air, she could pick out the melody.

Just as we had done in Tise when I was a child, so we did in Council Bluffs with Klara's family, Paul's family and neighbors, or church friends at the park or on the river-bank. At those outside events someone always had a guitar or banjo. Uncle Paul played the violin. Sometimes an Italian neighbor played the concertina with him. We sang and other times we danced. Anna showed her little sister how to hold a wide blade of grass between the forefingers and heels of both hands to blow a tune through it. Grass orchestras sounded pretty bad but that didn't matter al all. We had a wonderful time with it.

Ruth could see images and colors, although the only colors available to her were the brights, like red, orange and green. Those had to be fairly close to her face for detection. Some images were visible to her. If the light around an object was fairly bright then she could describe its general shape.

So the characters in my stories began to wear bright colors. These were different than the plainer version the older girls had heard about. Sounds, textures and smells began to appear, also. Sometimes, the telling halted temporarily for better explanations for Ruth. I enhanced the stories with emotion and great expression. All the senses found a new level inclusion in my stories so she could grow from the facet of that process.

"Momma, you never tell stories about the butterflies. I think they fly but I don't know for sure or anything else, like how big they are. Tell me about them. What color is a butterfly?"

CHAPTER SEVEN

Papa's School

The city of St. Louis developed out of and around the meandering Mississippi River as it ran in a more or less southerly direction toward the Gulf of Mexico. St. Louis business was born from the river, on both sides of the river, but the financial institutions, Union Station and other commercial enterprises already were centering on the west side of the river. In 1900 it was the fastest growing city in the west and the demand for housing stretched west from the river into the rich Missouri farmland. Already the city had more than 300 miles of electric street car lines to service that expansion.

The reward of Peter's long term dreams came with his acceptance into medical school in St. Louis, Missouri in 1900. By selling his interest in the store to his brother, Paul, we were able to open a rooming and boarding house on Jefferson Street, the street that ran due west from the Mississippi River.

The rooming house was a large three story structure, sitting close to the front walk, but with a large yard in the back. For the first time, we had an indoor toilet, not inside of the house, but in a tiny room on the back porch there was a toilet and small sink. The roomers and our family all used it. It was just as cold in there in the wintertime as our out-house in Council Bluffs, but at least we didn't have to walk through the wet rain or cold snow to reach it.

Preparation had begun for the World's Fair in 1904 and the demand for construction workers exhausted the local supply. Many men were recruited from other cities. Also St. Louis had become the largest port on the River. With the influx of outside workers, the need for housing was enormous. I had no trouble filling my house with roomers. Most of those boarded with me, also.

I had always been told I was a good cook, so, of course, I did most of the cooking. During the school year the girls all helped in the kitchen and by cleaning, laundry, changing the bed linens and so forth. Ruth was seven years old by then and of course, had her share of chores. There was a myriad of projects she was able to participate in, but her principle chore was the dish-washing. And she let us all know, Ruth did not like to do dishes. But she did them, anyway. She was a useful, needed member of our family and made an equal contribution to this important phase of our family's life.

During the summer, when school was not in session and when the crops were produced, all four of the girls helped in the food production. We had a garden in the rear yard. Papa helped there when he could but we raised about every kind of vegetable we could use on the dining table, carrots, potatoes, onions, tomatoes, squash, spinach and green beans. In addition to the girls preparing the soil, planting, watering and otherwise caring for the garden everything that couldn't be eaten at the time in our weekly meals, was canned for winter use. I made jellies and jams, and other condiments such as chow-chow, pickled gerkins and bread and butter pickles. The girls often went out to the farms to pick peaches and various fruits for canning for the winter. My kitchen most literally hummed for everyone but Peter helped. We sang and laughed and tricked each other and sampled our products, too. Keeping Peter in medical school was a family project and everything any one of us could do to reach his goal was done in good nature. We were all useful and needed.

On the surface, Ruth's sight limitations were no different than any other minor physical handicap. That is to say, since she started out her life with this condition, she had no expectations above what abilities she possessed. For the purposes of our efforts to make her a well adjusted child, Peter and I attempted to treat her as if she had total sight. Of course, we always had the sight problem at the back of our minds, but we tried to raise her just the way the other girls were raised.

Each of our girls had her duties for there was plenty to be done. Just from a stand-point of quantity we did laundry two or three times a week, depending on the weather, of course. The older girls carried out the baskets of wet clothes and Ruth could help hang them up by standing on a stool that Peter had built for her. In the wintertime, the basement furnace helped in the drying process. I was concerned about her safety around the hot furnace, so she wasn't allowed in the basement. She did the dusting and set the dinner table and other small chores like that.

There was an adjustment needed in moving away from the only house Ruth had known. She walked with hands outstretched, avoiding the bumps and knocks, hoping to find the corner before her head reached it. She groped her way around, holding to the railing when moving up and down the stairs. Sometimes, a thoughtless roomer left a suitcase in the middle of the hall or other unlikely place and Ruth took a tumble.

We didn't see Peter much. His days and nights were full and he often stayed at the hospital. All of us missed the more carefree days in Iowa, Peter's bass contribution to our singing and whist playing in the wintertime. It was easier for me when I kept the end result in my mind. In the last year, I counted the days when his training would be over, when we could all be together at least on Sundays and in the evenings.

He never seemed to overtire or discourage, even though he was older than the other students. He was nearing fifty by this time. I was always asleep when he climbed into bed with me but usually a gentle kiss awakened me and he had so much to tell me.

The children in St. Louis weren't as pleasant as Council Bluffs. Occasionally, my girls would be taunted about their immigrant parents. Of course, in Iowa, almost everyone was an immigrant. My girls' clothes were "home-made" and their "mother ran a rooming house." All these things made us second-class citizens according to the children. This kind of prejudice was of concern but I explained to the girls that it was only words, empty words. It meant nothing. To myself I wondered if these beliefs came from their dinner table, from their parents. Where had they learned those thoughts?

Our lives weren't all work. There was time in each of us to pause and enjoy our lives. There was a six year old boy next door who played with Ruth sometimes and he played well. But there were times when he'd have a friend with him and then the two of them played cruel tricks on her, such as tip-toeing up to the back of her and pushing her down. Our street had a lot of traffic, noisy enough to prevent her hearing their steps. She was particularly upset about it this one day so I kept her in. There were play-times when she would cooperate in a game in which her handicap was a part of the game and it was all right with her. There was a strong difference with these two boys for she thought she was being made fun of and tricked in an evil way. We talked about it, Ruth and I. She cried to let me know the depth of her hurt and after the tears had dried, she said, "Mama, I wanta be just like everybody else. Why do they treat me different?"

School was about to start and she would enter for the first time. Ruth came down with German measles. She recovered and we were making preparations for her to go to school when she got the flu. After that, it was a bad cold, then the mumps. I decided to postpone her entry into school for the balance of that year. That was a difficult year for Ruth because all her sisters were in school. She was able to do more of the chores during this time. It was badly needed and she wanted to be useful.

Even though the Missouri School for the Blind was easy to reach from the rooming house, all students had to live at the school, at least during the week. For the first time in her life, Ruth had to live apart from the rest of our family. Peter was able to take some time away from the hospital for Ruth's registration, so the three of us caught the 'E' line, right in front of our house, for the original trip to school.

On the first day of school, she bounced around in an effervescent joy. But as soon as the three of us got on the street-car Ruth became silent. I noticed her movements became more cautious and pensive. Peter was usually rather quiet and studious, but seeing Ruth's sullen face he entered into a running line of descriptive dialogue.

"What a great day this is! I remember my first day in school up on the Isle in Denmark. The school was a long way from our house and there were no street-cars in those days. My papa took my brother and me to school on the back of his horse. And then the school was only one room. Seventeen of us were all in that one room. That school had a bell on top of the roof and it rang for school to start. When it rang in the morning, we ran so we could be inside the door by the time it stopped ringing. We couldn't be late or we'd have to stay after class."

Ruth listened and became absorbed in the events of her father's childhood. The street car stopped directly in front of the school, for there were several families with students aboard. The school was a three storied building of dirty, red brick exterior, sitting on a very large plot of ground and included several out buildings of various sizes, several in brick, one of stone and two of frame construction. I presumed one of the other brick buildings was the superintendent's residence, for I was told he and his family lived at the school. Others "are probably workshops and storage buildings," Peter speculated. A great, long covered porch surrounded the front door. The windows were very narrow in relation to their height and the roof was made of thick, hand-made shingles. A fence of native stone enclosed the back half of the lot from the main building and the enormous area of playgrounds that stretched across the rear of the property.

Peter described it in full detail to Ruth, as we walked up the front walk. When his voice stopped, Ruth asked, if that was all.

"What do you mean, Porkchop? Should there be more?"

"Papa, where's the bell? Doesn't my school have a bell like Mama's old school?"

"Well, let me see. Why . . . yes. There is a bell up there. Sure enough, your school has a bell, too." He chuckled, "I guess all schools, worth anything at all, have to have a bell."

It was still late August, hot and very humid. It was early morning I carried a pink parasol for use after the sun became too uncomfortable. I wore my Sunday dress of peach voile. Peter remarked that I was the loveliest mother there, with my pastel colors and blue eyes. Ruth wore her best dress for that first day of school also, a mid-calf length dress of pale blue georgette with a round neck trimmed with white piping. She had an inset of white lace which circled her neck, matched by an inset of lace at the bottom of each of the gathered sleeves. It was her only good dress and was made for her by Anna. She wore white stockings, too warm for that time of year but necessary for the proper covering. On her feet were her only pair of shoes, a well polished, sturdy, pair of brown oxfords. Inger had helped with her hair that morning. Ruth could comb her own and braid it by herself. She was learning to place a tie at the end. For special occasions, and this was a very special occasion, Inger set her hair the night before and combed her blond hair into long, narrow, ringlets of curls with the two sides pulled to the back and tied with an oversized light, blue ribbon. From the front, the bow seemed to widen her ears, but from the back, the bow divided her long, yellow locks with the same color and fabric as her dress. When she first appeared before her father, she had danced and twirled to show the spread on her round, full skirt and then collapsed in giggles into his lap. Peter and I exchanged quiet smiles as we responded to her joy.

With so many others around now, she was again, quiet and pensive. The new students were to come at eight o'clock while those who had been pre-registered from last year didn't need to come until after lunch. However, some had already arrived. Peter thought those larger children playing outside might have come from the outlining areas of the state. Some still older children, in their teens, were standing about, idly talking. From what Peter could hear, they had known each other before.

We were surprised to be told by the man waiting ahead of us in line, that some of these older children were first year students. "Diseases and accidents can occur at any age," he said. "Several of these children come from down state, country areas and some from Ward schools. (Ward schools are public elementary schools.)

They transferred when their eyesight deteriorated, either gradually or suddenly, to reach that degree of deficiency which makes this school serve them better," as so stated by a well dressed gentlemen, with pince-nez glasses, standing ahead of us in the line.

As they edged forward toward the registration desk, Peter watched the children move about. He observed a different pattern of behavior in those young ones standing in his line, and he presumed they had never been to school. I noticed the older children walked erect, heads held level and steady and generally faced forward. This was also true of the children standing about, who had been there to school before. Most of the students whom we felt had never been to any school were timid, withdrawn, their bodies sometimes recoiled, weaving and rocking with their heads tilting in strange angles. Some were nervously tapping the walls with their knuckles. Not all the new children behaved this way. Most did.

"What made the difference?" Peter asked aloud, in an abstract way as though he didn't expect an answer.

Many children, having come from outlying towns and rural areas of the state, would have to spend their weekends here at the school. "Thank goodness, we live in town," I whispered to Peter, just as we reached our turn at the registration desk.

The young woman behind the desk introduced herself as Miss Murphy and confidently put her hand out straight ahead of her, although she slightly missed her mark, as it pointed pretty evenly between Peter and me. Peter was the first to take it.

"I'm Mr. Christensen and this is my wife." I shook her hand as he continued. "This is our daughter, Ruth. She's seven years old and this is her very first day at school."

Miss Murphy's eyes looked natural, except that she failed to move to follow her subject. It was hard to tell if she could see anything at all. She bubbled with exuberance and laughed with a light and friendly joy. I thought her personality was quite appropriate for this first contact with the school. She relaxed all of us as she took down the particulars of our daughter by way of a typewriter. When finished, she carefully removed the paper from the typewriter. She firmly gripped it with both hands so that the last part of the page out of the typewriter, remained on the bottom of the document as she turned it to us for signing. She set it squarely in front of Peter.

Peter curiously looked to see that the printing on the page and the typing this blind woman had made, were in perfect alignment, and sure enough, the typing was perfect and the line for his signature was at the bottom of the page. He turned to look at me.

After he signed, and handed it towards Miss Murphy, she took it and moved it close to her face, to be sure the printing was on the front. She then turned slightly to her left and put the form into a small metal slate, and began to duplicate the information on this new student, this time in Braille. She had remembered it all except she transposed two of the three numbers in the telephone number, but questioned in advance to entering that number the second time.

"Impressive! She remembered everything, almost And now any one can read the forms, blind or sighted." Peter seemed absorbed in her efficiency. He felt more at ease about the school when he made note of her skill.

After that was complete, all three were directed into a large room with chairs in rows in two sections. In just a short time, the superintendent, Mr. Woolly, came in the greet the new students. He began. "This school has been here since 1876. Since that time we've grown in our numbers and in our experience in this task. We've had the time to make some mistakes, correct them, and go on to make some more mistakes," (pause, and people laughed.) "But we've learned and gone on to develop methods for education of the blind that we feel are pretty unique in this country. We think we're among the best.

"Special attention will be devoted to your childs' physical development, teaching him to walk, how to use his hands to eat, bathe and dress just like with two good eyes. He'll romp out of doors, engage in the sports and pastimes of seeing, and have the bearing of the seeing. Your child, to be more specific, will look at the person to whom he's addressing. He'll avoid idiosyncrasies like weaving his body, turning in his toes or stooping his body. He or she will observe the laws of cleanliness and good health and participate in household duties."

Ruth already does those things, I thought and looked at Peter giving me a nod.

He continued. "We'll insist on quick obedience, strict honesty, truthfulness and purity. We'll excuse no violation of these values due to his infirmities."

"Papa, what does infirmisties mean?" Ruth whispered.

Leaning over to Ruth, he very quietly said, "because you don't have good eyesight. Hush, now."

"After this day you will never hear it said here that your child does not see. It is often said on the outside, indeed many think your child does not see. That is ad- herently false!" his voice rising slightly but emphatically. Then a pause for the drama of a southern preacher, and then spoke so softly we had to strain to hear, "And this is very important for you to understand, you and your other children and family members at home, must nev-ver, never suggest that your child does not see. Vision is impaired, and it is true, that their eyes do not see many things, some eyes see not at all. But all of them see in other ways."

The room was quiet, except for a slight bump of a swinging foot on the wooded chair leg. I glanced at Peter. I could tell he liked what he was hearing. Mr. Wooley continued.

"Seeing is understanding. There are many ways to understand, although those of us who are used to a good pair of eyes view the world from a 'quick look.' Here at this school, a 'quick look' comes from handling a new object in our hands, and then our 'quick look' actually becomes much more informative than the 'quick look' by the eyes of a person with clear vision. When the object is examined with the hands, one understands so much more. The temperature of the object, its size, the approximate weight, texture, flexibility, the moving parts, if any, and many other things that most of us sighted persons guess, with less accuracy, when we give it our kind or 'quick glance.'

"Your children will learn as they are just like everyone else except that their eyes cannot perceive as many others can. Everyone of us has something about him that may be different than the next person. Your child will see by smelling, hearing and feeling. He or she is different only to us with perfect, or near perfect vision, or to those of your children who at one time in their lives had excellent and normal vision. We will all work together to teach your child, not only how to live in our world, both socially and economically, but how to make a difference in the world.

"You parents are vital to these goals. Write often. Fill your letters with sunshine, love and hope for a successful, happy life. We cannot fail. Together," his voice dropped, as he began to wind down.

"My office is open to you at any time to discuss your child's progress and development. Let me know of any problems and I'll notify you if we have any here."

"And now, please join us for refreshments," nodding and pointing with his head toward the covered table by the windows. The room broke in a buzz of voices all talking at once. Coffee smells permeated the room and I could see a punch-bowl and large plates of cookies sitting at the edge of the table.

"Thank you, ladies and gentlemen, for your kind attention, and once again to you students, welcome!"

People clapped. Peter looked over at me, tightened his lips as he gave an approving nod. We stood up and began to move toward the refreshment table. Ruth did not weave her body or toss her head about like some of the other children. Peter thought about this and then he said. "I figure that's because Ruth can see some light and therefore, she is trying to make out images from the ground up. Those children who rock and bounce their heads back and forth are the ones with no sight at all."

In ten minutes, Miss Murphy came over to us with another little girl in hand, about the size and age of Ruth. She introduced Lena to the three of us and then told us that Lena would be Ruth's roommate and would take Ruth up to her room. This was Lena's second year at school, so she already knew the school well, and according to practice, she was placed in a sleeping room with a new student, in order to ease the way as much as possible for the new student.

Peter hoisted the valise of his daughter's belongings, and we followed the girls. We walked behind quietly as we listened to the girls talking. This was Ruth's first school friend. It was all quite new. But she liked her new friend already and for the present time, her new friend was her teacher.

As they headed out of the meeting room, hand in hand, they stopped in the doorway and Lena said.

"Now look at the doorway." Taking Ruth's hands, Lena quickly stretched her arms out to place each hand on separate sides of the door opening. "This particular room has a wide opening with two large doors. See, one opens this way" and pulling her to the other side of the doorway, "this one opens this way. They're big doors, aren't they?"

"Uh-huh!" Ruth agreed.

"Usually, only one of these doors is open but since so many people are here today they have them both open. For the moment, try to make your steps all the same size so you can figure out how to get around here by yourself. Taking your normal steps, let's count them from this door to the stairs. Walk just like you usually do. Now, the stairs are at the left of this doorway. Let's turn left. Do you think you have your bearings?" she asked Ruth. And then breaking her train of thought, "You do know your left from your right, don't you, Ruth?"

Ruth stiffened and pulled her chin up. "Sure," she said almost in defiance. Her brow furrowed.

"I thought you did," Lena said. "We can follow the wall on your left, until you can get used to this place. So, you touch the wall, Ruth." Lena stretched Ruth's arm over so her hand could touch the wall. "There's no furniture in this hall so once you get your bearings you can sail around here all by yourself. Let's count your steps. One, two, three, four," and so on to" twenty one steps to the stairs." They stopped momentarily. "Okay, Ruth, you got it?" she asked.

"Yes, twenty one steps to the stairs," Ruth said.

"Going up the stairs, we stay on the right side, always. Coming down, also stay to the right so you won't bump into anybody going the other way. Remember the right side is different coming down. It's on the other side."

Ruth interrupted. "We have stairs at home, but they're not this wide. Sometimes a boarder's on the stairs at the same time and he's always passed me on my left if he's going the other way."

"Good," Lena said. "We're already ahead of this game. I can see you'll know this place in no time."

Ruth grinned with the compliment.

Lena continued. "There are twelve steps to the landing, stay close to the banister and let it guide you, up and around to the next flight of stairs, Another twelve steps to the second floor."

Ruth asked, "Are we at the top?"

"Oh no, we're only up to the second floor where all the girls live. There is a third floor about us. That's where all the teachers live. The boys live in the basement." She continued, "the first floor has all the classrooms, the library and Mr. Wooley's office, and the second is where we stay. Also some of the women teachers have their rooms on our floor."

Ruth was fairly quiet, concentrating as she counted the steps at every change. Peter winked at me as we watched from behind the girls. At the top of the second flight of stairs, Lena stopped and continued. "Now, follow directly to your right and see how the banister railing blocks off this floor to the one below. I'll show you the marker for the beginning of the stairs down, when we go down. But now, follow the banister to the wall and then follow the wall to each door." We all walked as instructed. Lena continued.

"Now count the doors to number seven and that's our room." Lena had dropped Ruth's hand at the top of the stairs and let her move about on her own. Some doors were open and some were closed, but when Ruth reached the seventh door, she stopped and asked.

"Is this it? This is the seventh door. It this our room?"

"It sure is. Very good." Lena said, and noticing that Ruth's fingers had stopped at the wall at the entrance to the room, she said. "Do you see that little name-plate in Braille. Its framed in metal? That's my name. Yours will be up there with mine by the end of the week. So if you get mixed up you can find your room on your own. You'll soon be able to read your name."

Just inside the room, Ruth hesitated and moved ever so slowly, with her body just slightly bent forward as she searched for the way. She had always walked this way in new territory, groping and investigating as she moved forward.

Inside the seventh, Lena made no effort to lead Ruth through the room. She relaxed in her exercise and proceeded to let Ruth move through the room, until she found a bed. Then she told her that was her own bed. It was a small cot in one corner of the room. Lena's cot was in the opposite corner with the window in between. There was no closet. A four drawer dresser was against the wall next to the door.

"The two lower drawers are yours. I have the top."

At the foot of each bed was a small, rather crudely made table. It could be a stool for sitting, a writing desk, or could hold books or other necessities. Shoes were placed under the bed at night. A coat tree stood directly in front of the window, dowels on all four sides.

As Ruth reached the coat tree in her examination of her room, Lena said. "The two hooks on the back and side closest to your bed are for you to hang your things on, and the others on the front and my side are the pegs that I use."

Ruth sniffed and flared her nostrils, head back slightly. "I smell lavender. Where is the lavender?"

"My mother sent it back to school with me. She thinks my room smells nicer with lavender," Lena answered.

I joined in. "If you'd like, Ruth, remind me to bring in some rose petals for you to bring back with you after next weekend. Your room could begin to smell like a garden," I laughed.

Behind the coat tree was a steam radiator, and still behind, was one of the tall, narrow windows I had seen from the outside as we walked up the front walk. The room was dark but clean. The beds were simple, wooden cots with thin metal slats holding a four inch cotton mattress. A crisp, white pillow was at the head. I had brought one of her heavy quilts from home, partly unfolded it and placed in at the foot of her cot, even though it was too early in the year to expect to use it in the evenings. The walls hadn't been painted for many years and the floors were bare, both in and outside the rooms. Nothing indicated that the room was unkempt, except for the window that needed washing and for the area around the entrance that was at the place where the hands of a six year old of normal height would touch. I was used to those little finger smudges.

The building was old, even without the extravagance of the indoor toilet at the rooming house. A chamber pot sat under each girl's bed and every morning each girl had to empty her own into a pail. A black lady did the cleaning and it was her job to carry the enamel pail of human discharge down to the garbage area. From there, one of the maintenance men took it all way down below the farm area to a compost bin. After it was seasoned, or left for a period to de-compose, it was used for the garden which supplied the school with its vegetables for the year.

At the end of the second floor were two rooms with a single bathtub in each and several sinks. Ruth never used the bathtubs at school. She didn't need to since she went home every week-end. She took her weekly bath at home in the one tub up on the second floor. Everyone used the same tub at home, and everyone on the same floor at school used the same tub. During the week, she took "bird baths." That was what we called washing with a basin or water, soap and washcloth. Several of the girls used the bathroom at the same time for this ritual.

Leaving our younger daughter for the first night away from home was harder on Peter and me than it was for Ruth. She was already at home. She felt the pillow, the size, the softness, put it up to her nose to smell it. She was a year older than most of the children coming into the school for the first time. I began to feel sad when the time came for us to leave.

When Ruth and I hugged each other, Ruth began to get emotional. But Peter put his large arms around us both and said, "Now, my little pork-chop, we're right here in the same town, just a few blocks away and," hearing Ruth's giggles at his calling her 'pork-chops', he stopped. By that time, I'd started to laugh, too. Peter quickly pulled me out by the hand, knowing we needed to leave quickly. Our daughter was in good hands with the young Lena. We said "Good-bye," as we walked out the door. Lena was already telling Ruth about her favorite teacher.

"You'll like her, too. I know you will. But, then there's the old grump."

I don't think either knew when we'd left.

Weekends at home were the times for tub baths, hair washing and clothes washing. Ruth still always did the dishes, too, some of which were saved from the day before. Most of the clothes had to be starched. Then, they had to be ironed before she left again for the Sunday night trip back to the school, either one of her sisters or I ironed her blouses and dresses. All the tablecloths and napkins were easy enough for her to do, if there was time. Ironing took time, too, because the flat-irons had to be heated on the hot kitchen stove. When they became too cool, we replaced it with another hot one. That was a miserable job in the hot and humid days, but as the days grew cooler the chore became more tolerable. It was hard work, something Ruth could do and there was never an assumption that she was not capable for any reason. Unless, of course, she was sick.

She only had two jumpers and two white blouses. For rough play, she wore a full panted, knee length garment. One stayed home and the other went to school with her. In the winter time she wore black stockings that came just above her knee, ending just underneath her playsuit. In the springtime she wore white stockings. She didn't go to school in the summertime for when the weather turned hot and humid, school was out and Ruth was at home. She didn't wear stockings at all then. Anna had made her a sort of valise from a worn-out quilt. It had a rope closure with a loop on the end. Each week-end, that valise took the dirty clothes home and brought the clean and ironed ones back on Sunday night.

There were new people to meet, some were very nice and others she didn't like so well. One of the boys in the dining could see better than Ruth and in the beginning, he would sit close to Ruth. If the dessert was a particularly good one, at least one that he liked, he's tell Ruth there was something floating in her dish.

"Maybe a bug" or "a black something" and he'd "be happy to help her out by removing it." Ruth gladly accepted his willing assistance in this, until she realized each time there was snickering from the others, and then her desserts were always so small. Then, when she verified the real story with Lena, Lena told her that her dessert friend was really a dessert pirate of infamous reputation at the school. He had long gorged himself on as many desserts as he could steal from the gullible At that Ruth vowed to rid herself of his thievery.

She enlisted the help of the cook, who told her they were having strawberries for supper the next day. Her friend had limited sight. So sure enough the next evening the bowls of bright red strawberries were floating in rich, fresh cream and one was delivered to each place at the table. He must have licked his lips for her thieving friend knew he'd be enjoying more strawberries than his own for this meal. He quickly ate his meal and dessert, and didn't even notice that Ruth was so busy talking and laughing that she hadn't even eaten half of her supper. He, again, made his generous offer to "clean up" her dessert so she could eat it, and she graciously accepted his kind invitation, telling him how glad she was that he sat next to her, and he was such a fine and helpful friend. In her most sincere voice, she buttered him well. "How can I ever thank you?" suppressing a giggle.

Lena knew Ruth had talked to the cook, but she gave no explanation except she made this one comment. "This supper will be interesting. Pay attention to what I am doing."

Lena suspected the interesting part might be related to the frequently stolen dessert. Both the cook and the dishwasher watched from the kitchen door, when the young man sugared and took his first bite of Ruth's strawberries. One bite, a cough and a yell. He sprayed his food out over the table and the students on the opposite side, with the half chewed strawberries from his mouth. He jumped up and ran out of the dining room, groaning and moaning. Ruth had asked the cook for powdered alum so she could sprinkle it on his berries. (I had used powdered alum for my pickling of cucumbers each summer and Ruth, always curious to know about everything, learned first hand when she sampled some of the white powder. Just a little bit makes the mouth feel puffy and the tongue almost paralyzed.

Ruth rolled in glee, and quickly, she told Lena exactly what she had done, who in turn, explained it to the others. The "puckered mouth" and bitter taste, kept the young man's hands on his own desserts from that point on.

At first, spelling was difficult for Ruth. As she had two parents at home who spoke with Danish accents, she was slower to correctly hear the words. But by the beginning of the second year, she spelled with one hundred percent accuracy and became a spelling bee contestant.

Numbers were only memorizing, also. That was easy. Learning to read was slow and tedious to begin with, but again, as soon as Ruth had memorized the six-point Braille system thoroughly, those courses were a little easier. She learned to read and write her name, but Ruth didn't begin studying Braille in earnest until the beginning of the second year. She loved going home on Friday nights, and telling and showing her family what she had learned.

Her family had participated in the teaching of so much, unlike many other families of children in her school who, out of their own ignorance, were simply 'putting the child on the shelf', not teaching him anything. Ruth was most able and self confidant. Her teachers were very complimentary in speaking of her progress to her parents. Although, her exercise class teacher did complain of her clowning in class and generally being noisy and disruptive.

Into her second year, the principle teacher told me that it had come to her attention that Ruth had exhibited an unusual musical talent. Of course, this came as no surprise to Peter and me. She said, it seemed that almost from the time she entered the school, each time she passed a practice room where a string player or other instrumentalist was rehearsing, she would open the door and correct their pitch. At first, the other students resented this smart-aleck, but when they realized that, by her correction they looked better to their teachers, they began to listen to her. As a matter of fact, some even invited her to come in about 10 minutes before their lessons began to help them "tune up". Some of their music coaches never knew.

The director of music became aware of her perfect pitch, when her strong voice began to sing a pitch, before he sounded the pitch on the piano or the pitch pipe. She reminded the director that the school's piano in one of the practice rooms needed tuning. No student of the second grade had ever shown that ability.

CHAPTER EIGHT

Life At The St. Louis School

Mama and Papa picked St. Louis as the best school for Papa to study medicine and just by luck they got the best school in the country for me, too. The Missouri School for the Blind had been the leading proponent of the punctiform method of reading for the blind in the entire world. That's a dot or series of dots, six in total, that are arranged differently for each letter in the alphabet. Punctiform was actually invented prior 1815 by an engineer looking for a military method of reading in the dark. He also considered it valuable for use as a secret code. Louis Braille chafed at the thought that he, as a blind man hadn't the ability to read music. So he arranged the dot system and presented it with enthusiastic response by the blind in England and France. However, sighted persons whose sense of touch was not as developed as the blind, trying to find sense from the arrangements of six dots in the Braille system, were very disinterested. Unfortunately these policy decisions about these most important issues were not made by the people who needed to use them but others who considered the blind of less than a capable mentality. The Missouri School embraced the Braille system like a long lost brother, needed and welcome into the community of learning, and actually spearheaded its use in this country.

Of course, at the time, I was too young to realize its value. It was many years later, when I realized just what the life of the blind had been before me, did I understand just how fortunate I was to live in this era and in this state.

From my point of view, I was in a dream world to be with other children who were just like me. Lena had said, "We're all being served from the same pot of soup." We all had some differences, of course. One came to notice within a few days after school started. I asked one of the girls next to me at supper one night, if she was afraid of the dark? At the time I didn't realize she was totally blind. She answered, "I don't know what you mean." Since I had light during the daytime and when the sun went down and the inside lights were turned off, then I had the darkness. So I had both light and darkness. With no sight at all she had only the dark.

For the first time in my life I had my own, my very own friend, unknown to my sisters and parents, and as time passed I got to know so many girls just like Lena, all right there at the school.

At home I probably worked much harder to show that I could do everything my sisters could do. Well, not in some ways, but I'd make up for the shortage by becoming better than my sisters in other ways. I could play with dolls just like them. Only, they were older and out-grew dolls before I did. But for instance, I couldn't play hop-scotch, or roll hoops or catch balls with them or the other children in the neighborhood. At home, Mama let me race my tricycle in the house but not out on the sidewalk. When Mama was away from the house or the window, I could climb the trees, at least some of them. The other kids in the neighborhood could ride both places and climb all the trees, but I really wanted to be able to do everything they could do. I wanted to be just like them.

At the blind school, we all played together and on an equal basis. There was a ball-game that some of us played together at school. We use a big ball, so big my arms couldn't reach around it. Inside the ball was a bell. The kids would kick the ball and we all ran to where we could hear the ring going. We had to find it and kick it back so there was a mad scramble to get to the ball and kick it. Well sometimes, there were a lot of legs to compete with and we had some really big collisions.

One time I got my arm cut when I hit a concrete wall. I could feel the warm blood rolling down my arm, so the game was called to a halt so I could get first aid. When my arm was patched we all went right back into the game.

But the very greatest and wonderful fun at that school was the Japanese swing. I had never seen one before and haven't since. Twelve or fourteen of us could swing at one time and we made a real party out of it. It was like a giant porch swing, except instead of the swing moving back and forth like a porch swing, this moved sideways. It had a very long bench, 12 or 14 feet long where everyone sat at the same time. That bench was cradled on an arm suspended by two chains from overhead bars, "well supported bars," Papa had said. We could make it swing very wide if we had a lot of kids riding on it. The little kids sat in the center of the board and the bigger kids stood on the ends and held on to the side chains, shifting their weight to change directions. When we were all swinging together higher and higher we played like we were on a school team. As we rolled into a roaring swing, we would start singing a "round," something we knew from class like "Scotland's Burning," or "Row, Row, Row your Boat." Each time another section of the round came in to sing, we tried to make it louder than the other, as the swinging got more robust. The swing was way down on the back lot so we never got in trouble for making too much noise. When the recess bell sounded, everyone groaned. It was such wonderful fun that none of us wanted that play to end.

I got very sick when I was nine years old. I had a high fever and stomach ache. Papa pressed my stomach to see if I might have appendicitis. I didn't. The next day, Inger came down sick, too. I overheard Papa tell Mama we might have "the fever," and so he had one of the other doctors from the hospital come by to see us. They diagnosed Typhoid Fever. This was hard on Mama. Exactly one week later Papa got sick, too. No one could come into our end of the house because Papa put us in quarantine. All our dishes were scalded in boiling water and so were all our towels and sheets. Papa said, "By the Grace of God Mama, Anna and Esther were spared. I don't understand it, but I give my thanks, anyway." None of the roomers got sick either.

Papa said a city up-river, Chicago, was dumping its garbage, human sewage, too, into the Illinois River, and that river ran into our river, the Mississippi. Our city drank from the river so it made so many people sick. Mama said Papa became the sickest. Inger lost all her pretty, black hair and when she got well, all her hair grew back the same color but this time it wasn't straight anymore. It was curly.

One morning after I got well it was still dark when I woke up. For a long time I laid there and listened. I could hear somebody in Papa's room. Mama always got up at five o'clock to set her bread for the day, and I could occasionally hear someone down in the kitchen. I assumed that had to be Mama, but the sun never came up. After a while I went to Papa's bedroom. He was feeling much better but he still hadn't fully recovered from the fever. I opened the door slowly, and said quietly, "Papa, 'you awake?"

"Well good morning, Pork-chop!" I knew then he was feeling better. "Yes, I'm awake and it looks like you are too." He continued. "How did you sleep?"

"Fine," I said, walking up close to lean against his bed.

"Is it still night-time, Papa?" I asked.

The white organdy sheers in the eastern window were always bright in the morning sun. This morning it was still dark. Papa began to laugh.

"Of course not, silly. Just look . . ." He stopped mid-sentence as he must have realized what I was really asking.

Very somber now, "What do you see, Ruth?"

"Night, Papa. Everything is black. Shouldn't the sun be out, yet?"

Papa told me it was daytime and that the sun was out.

"Why can't I see it, Papa. Why can't I see the light?" I didn't understand at all. "What has happened to the sun? The light is always there in the mornings. Even during a storm, it is always light. Where is it this morning?" I turned around to all directions and only saw darkness.

From that time on I never again saw light, any kind of light, not the light of the sun or the moving light of a fire. My world became black. I was afraid.

Mama said the light might come back but it didn't. Mama seemed to slip back into her depression after that. I believe that change in my sight upset her because when I'd talk to her she wouldn't answer, like she didn't even hear me. Sometimes she would answer me in a cross voice, like she was mad at me. She stayed off to herself a lot and otherwise was quiet unless speaking with someone else. It was a time after that she began to grow out of that depression and began to laugh like she used to most of the time.

I thought I had done something wrong. I could feel her tension and isolation but couldn't understand what it was. I fought with Inger a lot during that time. One day, I hit Inger and she slapped me back. Mama heard us.

"What is this?" she said she couldn't believe it. We never fought.

I was already crying and just burst out. "Nobody loves me anymore. You don't care what happens to me. I wish I was dead."

Both Mama and Papa told me they loved me but still they seemed very sad at times. It was like our house was covered with a lid of sadness. I longed for just a glimmer of light at some time, anytime, just for a moment, but it never came.

When I was ten, I knew that I could do things my sisters couldn't do. Mama said I had a sixth sense. She said everybody has five but I have six. I knew where the trees were when we all went fishing. I didn't have to touch them to know where they were, that is, if they were big trees not just twig-sized trees. Whether it was daytime or night time, whether the wind was strong or still, I could always tell if they were within 10 to 15 feet away from me. That sense worked not just for the trees but for buildings and houses. Papa helped me develop that sense because one time when we were fishing, he took me for a walk in the forest alongside of the river. We went alone and he sent me on ahead to test me as he watched from behind to make sure I didn't get into real trouble. He taught me to listen to every step and think about what I heard. Was it different from the last step, or the step before that? He told me to stoop down to see what was underneath my feet or what was around my feet.

"The sounds of a hard rock are very different from soft grass and tree leaves. Do you get any kind of an echo?" he asked. "What does it sound like to you?"

"Papa, do you hear the way our voices sound now from the way they sounded back when we started walking? There's more hollowness in your voice now. Do you hear that?"

"Now that you mention it, I do, Ruthie. But in order to really hear it everything must be very quiet, that is, no dogs bouncing around or sisters yelling. Wait! I see a break in the trees. Let me go ahead and see what's there."

I waited just a couple of minutes for him to move past me and walk several steps ahead. He stopped and yelled back with an even deeper voice that reminded me of the noise made from a big bassoon in our school orchestra. "We're at a turn in the river, Ruthie, and the bank lowers itself into the water right ahead. The path turns around it. What does that mean to you?"

"With the bank lowering into the river down there that explains why the sound changes. The echo is even hollower now that you are right at the edge 'cause the space below is bigger. So anytime I'm walking and I notice the deeper echo, I better stop to make sure I don't fall or get into trouble."

In time with these exercises I found out that dampness changed the sounds too. If it was raining, the sound of my feet on a sidewalk or on dirt or grass, were muffled. I noticed the chirp of the crickets changed to a different tonal pitch just before a rain or a change in the weather.

Before I had typhoid fever, I didn't think much about my eyes. It was only once in a while that one of us talked about how much we could see or couldn't see. One time, when two of the big boys just had a wild idea, they jumped on a bike together. It was just a sudden decision to take a ride. They headed down hill on the sidewalk close to the street. Johnny burke was riding on the tandem rail and Allen Downey was on the seat holding the handlebars, guiding them and pumping the pedals.

John suddenly yelled out, "Isn't there a big tree along here somewheres?"

"Yeah! Tell me where it is?"

Allen quickly called, "Boy, can't you see where it is? You do see, don't you?"

"No, I thought you . . ." and just then they hit the tree just right of the center of the handlebars and each boy went flying off in two directions. It may have killed them had the tree been in the middle of the sidewalk, and even then, Allen was out cold for several minutes. The school nurse told them they must have hard heads because they could have gotten hurt real badly.

Some of my independence was lost after the fever. Sometimes, I would wake up thinking it was time to get outta bed when it really was still in the middle of the night. At the school there was no problem because a bell rang when it was time to get up but at home I waited for the sound of several feet or move on out floor and then I knew it was time.

At the St. Louis school, I had almost two years of piano lessons. I loved playing and when I was home, Mama never had to tell me to practice. I could hear a tune and play it by ear. Some of Mama's roomers would test me by singing a new song. If they could sing in tune, I could always play the song.

Mama made the best apple pies. I could tell the kind of pie because of the smell. She only put cinnamon and nutmeg in the apple pie but the pumpkin pies, beside having cinnamon and nutmeg, also had ginger. Christmas vacations were three weeks long and Mama let me bake cookies and help with the special treats that had to be made in advance. No one but Mama made the fruitcakes, and they were done weeks in advance with a "secret" ingredient. It wasn't secret to me though because I could smell it when she was making the batter. When she opened the bottle I knew. It was Papa's home brew that she added. She wanted it to be a secret because our minister said liquor was wrong. Papa made it and he drank it. The cakes were stored in the cellar to "season", Mama said. (Papa made his homebrew every year. Nobody liked to drink it in our house but him, and he really seemed to enjoy it.)

By the time I was nine years old, Mama let me make shortbread. After that, gingerbread. I copied the recipes in Braille, so except for getting down the ingredients from the shelves that were taller than I, I could do it all myself. I could smell the spices to tell them apart. The sugar was in a different sized can than the salt and I memorized the different sized measuring spoons and cups. Afterward, Mama used to tease me about the way her kitchen looked. She would laugh and say a tornado had just passed through her kitchen. I knew she didn't mind if I made a mess.

When Christmas vacation was over that year, I returned to school, but Lena stayed home with the flu. That night would be the first time I had ever slept all alone in a room by myself. "But that's all right. I'm getting bigger and I can do more things by myself, now." I said proudly.

Mama and Papa had taken me back to school in Papa's buggy. Mama had packed me a basket of Christmas goodies, dried fruit, nuts and cookies in a tin. I hid them all in my drawer, under my clean underwear and stockings. The first night went well, although it was awfully quiet there my myself. Even when Lena was there, her breathing made a little noise. I missed her. I stayed awake for a while after I went to bed. The floor creaked when somebody walked down the hall. I began to count the horses by the clopping racket as they moved down the street in front of the school. Sometimes it was a single animal with a rider and other times there were more horses pulling a wagon or buggy. I figured out if the wagons were loaded by the way the wheels moved on the ride. Eventually, I dropped to sleep.

On the afternoon of the second day, I seemed to be starving and I remembered Mama's cookies. I took two out and was almost finished on the first one when we were called to dinner. The second cookie, I quickly stuffed under my pillow.

After dinner I went into the practice rooms to work on a new Chopin's Etude. When I went upstairs, I noticed nothing unusual in the activities on my floor. Some of the girls moved in and out of the bathrooms to their rooms, but that was down at the end of the hall. As I passed some of the rooms, I could pick up some bits of conversation and I stopped at one door to see what they were laughing at. But it was close to curfew so I needed to get on to my own room.

When I went into my and closed the door, I sensed something was wrong. It was nothing I could put my finger on. I wasn't scared but I was really wary. I stopped, stood very still and listened closely for the something or someone in the room with me.

WHAT COLOR IS A BUTTERFLY | 91

WHAT COLOR IS A BUTTERFLY | 91

"Who's there?"

No response.

There was no noise. Maybe I was mistaken. Sometimes, being alone makes me imagine things, like when the wind blows the trees against the house. It could be a cat scratching to get in. There was no sound, at least, not identifiable and it was so quiet it was almost imperceptible. Could it be termites in the walls? Mama, always says you can hear termites when they chew the wood.

As I moved, the room became completely silent. I threw off my clothes and quickly pulled my flannel night gown over my head. There it was again. I stopped, rigid. What was it?

"Who's in here?"

No answer, only silence. Maybe it was only my imagination. Did all girls sleeping alone for the first time "think" they heard noises? I asked myself.

Maybe I should open the door to the hall. I'd not feel so alone if I could hear someone out in the hall. I opened the door, turned and as fast as I could, charged the bed, grabbing the top edge of the covers, tossing aside my pillow in one action and threw myself at the bed.

Then it ATTACKED. Something hit me on my arm, cutting my hand. It was warm and furry. It virtually flew at me, sinking razor-sharp teeth into the soft tissue of my hand between my thumb and forefinger. I pulled back in total terror, screaming in fear and pain. Warm blood ran surging from my hand. "Where was it?" "What was it?" "Is it going to hit me again?"

I ran screaming to the doorway, out into the hall, senselessly and frantically racing first one way and then the other. I was hysterical and in absolute terror. Only later did I realize I had heard the 'thud' from my attacker as it hit the floor, the "squeak" and the scratch of claw feet racing across the wooden floor to escape through the open door. The pain in my hand was excruciating.

Miss Minerva, our housemother, came running, racing down the hall toward the sound of my screaming. She caught me and lifted me right off my feet, hugging me and holding me tightly. As first she screamed back at me and then softened her voice as I relaxed in the security of her hold. She had encircled me with her arms and gently rocked me back and forth.

"Now, now. It's gone." She must have seen the blood rolling off my hand for she said, "You won't be hurt anymore. Come let's go downstairs to the infirmary and let Miss Ila take a look."

I whimpered, "Oh-o-o-o, it hit me. It bit me. It jumped at me. What was it? Why did it hurt me?" She pressed her handkerchief hard where my hand was bleeding. She ignored my questions and just tried to soothe me. But afterwards, she told me she had seen an enormous rat running in the hall away from my room. Mama and Papa came to the school when the nurse called them. Papa said he was concerned that the rat was mad, and even though my hand was painted with iodine and wrapped, blood still seeped through the bandage. Papa took another look and then took me to his hospital. He said the rat's long, chewing teeth cut deeply into my hand and so the doctor at the hospital took some stitches

"How could it get into my room, Papa?"

"Rats are a big problem in this city. They come in by boats from Italy and Asia and other far-away places. When the ships are unloaded there's nothing left for the rats to eat, so they come ashore looking for food. Then, from there they go inland to find more food. Meantime, they have families and with more babies to feed they need more food."

"But I don't have any food, Papa. Why did he bite me?"

"I think you did have food, Ruthie. There were cookie crumbs on your bed. That rat wanted your cookie."

Papa was quiet for a moment and then said, "I'll have to talk with the school about this."

I went home with them that night. Mama and Papa refused to let me go back to school after that. Papa would soon complete his medical training and we'd be leaving St. Louis for a new life in a new town.

The next Sunday afternoon, Papa and I were alone in the parlor and he called me over to the settee next to him.

"Ruth," he said, "you told your mama that you thought something was wrong when you went into your room on the night the rat bit you. Is that right?"

"Yes, Papa. I may have heard him move or something, but I just knew that I wasn't alone in that room. I was sure of it."

"Well, that rat was probably surprised that you interrupted his meal. Usually, they'll run away from a person. They will, unless they're cornered. And I think that's what you did when you tried to get into your bed so quickly. Next time you have those feelings, know that you are probably right about a problem. Back off and be sure." He pulled me close and wiped the stray hairs back from my forehead. I could feel his breath on the side of my face. "I think when you lost your sight, God replaced that loss with another gift, a special gift. That gift is there to protect you and keep you safe. You're pretty accurate in those hunches that you get once in a while. And I want you to pay close attention to them, always."

"But I was all by myself. I didn't know it was there. I couldn't see," I whined.

"None of us can see in the dark. And there'll be many times you'll be by yourself. Think about it. You can protect yourself by what you do next. Just get the house-mother. That's what she's there for. Ask her to come in for a minute. Find someone who can see to come in and look around your room. Those people are there to take care of you and that's very important to your mama and me. Understand, Pork-chop?"

"Yes, Papa." He kissed me on the cheek and patted my behind as I walked away. I knew Papa loved me.

*   *   *

For the rest of that school year, I stayed home and helped Mama with the rooming house. I continued to practice on the piano regularly often to an audience of roomers entering and exiting the house. Sometimes they would simply pause in the hall for a few minutes. Other times they would sit down in the parlor to listen for awhile once they had checked for Mama's approval. I always was aware someone was in the room but it was like a background screen that was simply there in the room. I played on concentrating on learning the notes, giving it a different rhythm or trying out ways of giving it more expression. I was pretty good even then and often the roomer would clap or slip away, sometimes giving Mama a compliment about me.

Papa said he talked to "everyone" knowing he would soon finish school and need to move to where he could open his practice and make a living. One of his requirements was a proximity to a school for me. My sisters complained about the prospects of the move and "losing" their friends but readily acknowledging the need for a school for me. Papa wanted a town that was in need of his services, a town that showed promise for population growth for his future and that of his daughters financial future.

Arjenta in Arkansas was on the other side of the Arkansas River that bordered one side of Little Rock. It was a railroad town both in the number of rail-lines close-by and the manufacture and repair of locomotives, and it was growing. There was so much work there to attract the workers who then brought their families. A large number of Negroes lived in the area and worked either across the river or in Arjenta. Their income was lower than the whites which limited their ability to pay for medical care and some doctors refused to service the blacks. Many lived in the country and raised chickens and pigs and various crops. Papa figured he could barter his services for a chicken or eggs, etc. There weren't any Negroes in Denmark and he didn't recall any in Iowa either but he saw many Blacks in St. Louis and in Arkansas. They were still people and they needed medical attention just like everyone else.

After Papa made a trip there a month before graduation he learned the town had no doctor at all. He visited the Arkansas School for the Blind in Little Rock, spoke with the superintendent and toured the facility and learned the music department there was particularly good. He gave it his stamp of approval for me and then he found rental space above a corner grocery store in Arjenta.

After selling many of our furniture pieces we packed one wagon of our remaining goods, including our Reid organ, and sent it ahead to Arjenta with Mama's handyman. The family boarded the train for the trip to a new life for us all and we moved to Arkansas.

We moved into in the same building as Papa's office. The main entrance was by way of stairs leading up from the side street. That was the entrance to Papa's office. Two rooms in the front of the apartment were for his office. The balance was for us to live in and we had free entrance and exit out the back door off the alley just off the street. Papa soon traded his wagon for a buggy so he could make house calls in style. A wooden sign hanging over the door right on the street announced his services.

Arjenta had wooden sidewalks which was a great benefit in the rainy season. The dirt streets were dreadful in the wintertime when the wagons made deep ruts, often getting stuck in the mud where the traffic was heavy. We were just a block off the street car line allowing real convenience for the others girls in school or for moving about for church or work. The town was pretty wide open in early 1900's with lots of saloons and houses of "ill repute" as Mama explained.

By the end of the summer he had started to see several patients a week. By the end of the summer all of us were well entrenched into the Baptist church and I was ready to begin school in my new school.

CHAPTER NINE

The Move

The reason for our living in St Louis would soon cease as Papa would be completing his training and hopefully start to make a living in his long awaited field. He said he talked to "everyone" knowing he would soon finish school and needed to move to where he could open his practice. There was many criteria for a move, one principally was a close proximity to a school for me. My sisters complained about the prospects of the move and "losing" their friends but readily acknowledged the priority of a school for me. Papa wanted a town that was in need of his services, a town that showed promise for population growth for not only his future but for opportunities for his daughters. The entire country was spreading westward, developing and enlarging, improving and modernizing to a better life. There wasconsiderable attraction to the mechanized movement of the time, away from the small farms that worked its owners hard but did little else other than to sustain them and their families. After the great building boom to build the World's Fair in St. Louis was over many men were in need of jobs.

Other areas of the mid-states had more jobs than readily available men to fill. Arjenta, Arkansas was one of those cities. Advertisements were placed in the St. Louis newspapers boasting of Arjenta's job "opportunities" and inviting men to come to work there and bring their families. "Easy bank loans for any man with a regular paycheck", so the newspaper said. Of course Papa didn't yet have a regular paycheck but could easily speculate on the need for his services in an expanding town of already 12,000 and growing monthly. He expected his income to grow. Papa went to Arjenta to investigate.

Arjenta was in Arkansas, on the north side of the Arkansas River directly opposite Little Rock. These years were the era of the railroad in the great expansion westward and with the location of Arjenta close to the middle of the state it was a natural for commercial development around the use of the railroad. Crops needed to be sent out in all directions to near and far. The produce included cotton, cotton seed oil, fruit, vegetables, hay and rice. It was a railroad town both in the number of rail-lines running through and the service and repair of locomotives, blacksmith shops, mercantile stores, the South's largest cotton seed oil plant. Logs were floated down the river to be milled at the area's sawmills. There was so much work there to attract the workers who then brought their families. No fewer than four rail lines serviced the area already. There were general shops for the Mississippi Pacific Railroad that employed over 2500 men with a $2 Million a year payroll. The Rock Island Railroad employed about 700 workers. The most important point of all was in that year was the town had no physician.

Their were other fine points about Arjenta, such as a lovely park with a bridge over a lake, several churches and schools, although high school started in the fifth grade and went only to the tenth. There was a dance hall. It boasted "pure artesian water." The town had already developed from a bucket brigade fire department to a 120 pound pressure hose, the latest available. It even had both a fire and a police chief.

On the other hand there was no public water system, and only two lights existed on the entire streets of the town. The sidewalks were wooden plank and in the winter rains the horses and buggies and the work horses with wagons frequently got mired in the mud and sand. There was talk of drainage tiles to be installed soon.

Plans were already being drawn for a gas line to be built for the city and there were already 25 miles of sidewalks and 12 miles of sewer lines in place. But Papa failed to mention the number of barrel houses, actually there were 14 saloons. All the houses of prostitution already entrenched into the life of the city, but the commercial opportunities for him in that class didn't miss his consideration. He knew there were patients who needed his services in that profession.

Oh, there was a 9 o'clock curfew but the unsavory class ignored it altogether and the better citizens were happy it was there for their young people.

A large number of Negroes lived in the area and worked either across the river in Little Rock or in Arjenta. Their wages were lower than the whites which limited their ability to pay for medical care. For this reason some doctors refused to service the blacks, ignoring them altogether. Many blacks lived in the country and raised chickens and pigs and various crops. Papa figured he could barter his services for a chicken or eggs, etc. There weren't any Negroes in Denmark and he didn't recall any in Iowa either but he saw many blacks in St. Louis and in Arkansas. They were still people and they needed medical attention just like everyone else. He paid no attention to color.

Papa made the trip to Arjenta over a month before graduation, staying two days at the Duncum Hotel on Main Street. Before leaving St. Louis he visited with the school superintendent of Ruth's school to inquire about the Arkansas School for the Blind. He was told that state school was in Little Rock itself and included live-in arrangements for students who didn't live right there in the city. He also learned the music department in the Arkansas school was outstanding. That was good news. Papa was very encouraged after he visited the school in person on that visit. After giving it his stamp of approval for me he began looking for space for his office and living space for the family. He engaged space above a grocery store, about eight blocks from the horse and foot bridge across the river to Little Rock. The family and his patients could use the door directly off the street. Papa said nothing about the toilet arrangements until we moved in and discovered for ourselves the out-house in the rear yard. After the in-door toilet in St. Louis we were rather spoiled but readily regressed to a chamber-pot with a once-a-day dump to the outhouse. Here in this town Argenta had a weekly service to clean and spray the outhouses so at least that was better than in Council Bluffs. Whew!

We couldn't take all our belongings so we sold some things and packed two wagons with all the wicker furniture, Mama's pans and linens and some other special items, including our Reid organ. Mama's handyman and his son delivered them three days after we arrived in Arjenta. The family boarded the train for the trip to a new life for us all and we moved to Arkansas.

Papa soon traded his wagon for a buggy so he could make house calls in style and soon a wooden sign was hanging over the door right on the street announced his services. We were in a new life.

We all had the summer to set up our apartment, get settled in a new church and plan for the fall opening of the schools. Momma and Anna made new play clothes and a nice Sunday dress for me for I had almost outgrown all my clothes and generally got me ready for the school starting in the fall. Very early the family took a buggy ride from our apartment in Arjenta over into Little Rock just to see the town and the government buildings for it was also the state capital.

There was a school for the deaf and a separate school for the blind. The free bridge crossing the river was Main Street which was the direct route to the blind school on Main and 18th. The street car line ran down main street both in Arjenta and Little Rock. On that first trip Momma explained the route, what building were on the land, what they looked like, the color, construction material used, out buildings, bare land around and all pertinent information for me to get a mental picture of the city. It was much more developed than Arjenta, more paved streets and sidewalks and street lights. Most of the buildings were brick ... red brick with white trim. Some were wooden and those were all white in shades due to their age and wear. Some were set back from the street with many lovely shade trees in front, others closer to the street with only some bushes in front or just bare dirt.

When we got to 18th we turned west and then the school for the blind was on our left side. It, too, was red brick, two stories on top of a basement and a tower on a third floor over the entrance to the main building. It, too, had a bell in it, just like the St. Louis school. There were identical buildings on each side of the center structure, all had porches clear across the front. Several other buildings set back on the lot behind the front buildings with dirt roads leading from the street deep into the rear of the property. Papa said there were over 300 students at the school after he visited it in the spring and most of them stayed there throughout the week.

We got out of the buggy and walked back into the lot so Papa could tell me exactly what was back there. There were some garages up close to the street, but behind the front buildings there was a laundry, farm buildings and a house probably used by a staff person. There was a gym, play area of swings and base-ball diamond and vegetable garden. We didn't go back any further but we did walk all around the buildings so I could get a jump on familiarizing myself with the lay-out of the school. Occasionally we saw people around and we did meet the watchman who gave us his approval after Papa told him why we were there.

On the way home Papa told Momma that he had recently heard about artificial eyes made for people who had no vision at all. "It is purely for appearances, of course, but after prolonged blindness the eye-balls shrink, as Ruth's have done, and the glass eyes fit under the lids, giving the eyes a more normal shape. I've seen the colors available in them and they are as close to the colors of natural eyes as the real thing. They are very real looking."

Momma was thinking, "But it seems like they would be uncomfortable to wear, like they would scratch or cause the eyes to itch."

"They are completely smooth on the sides touching the eyeball and anyway, there is a lubricant to be applied before inserting the glass eye. And in any event the tear-ducts still work to further lubricate the eyes as needed."

"Can Ruth use them?" Momma asked.

"That, I'm not sure of. She has more growth coming and they're rather expensive anyway. Perhaps in a few years after she reaches her full growth and also is old enough to take care of the eyes, not lose them or break them, the time would be better for her."

Turning to me, he asked if any of my friends wear them and I told him I guessed not since I'd not heard of them before. Certainly I'd have heard the girls talking about them. I wasn't sure I wanted them. My eyes had a certain amount of itching anyway and glass eyes, or any foreign object might make it worse. Anyway, I let the subject end right then and there.

CHAPTER TEN

The Black Widow

When school started after summer was over, I was ten years old. Papa's information on the school about the outstanding music teacher was good information. I adored Professor Trebing. Most of the teachers were alright but I related particularly well to my music teacher. However, I had to take a sewing class "to prepare for future needs," according to my sewing teacher, Miss Simm. I really don't think any of us considered being be a professional seamstress, but I can understand the need to replace missing buttons and the like. Those of us capable of college, or more likely, whose parents were rich enough to send us to college, were put into advanced literature, geometry and classes like logic and public speaking. Grace and I were both among those. Others had a greater aptitude for manual shop, broom-making, fabric and rug weaving, mattress making, or piano tuning and repairing. But all girls had to take the sewing class.

The very first day we looked at the different thicknesses of the threads and yarns, and the kind of needles to be used with them. She told us to find the thickest part of the needle, and the flat side that housed the hole. That was easy to feel. Then came the hard part. We had to learn to thread the needle.

Miss Simm explained. "The end of the thread requires a clean cut thread so it can enter the eye of the needle more easily." We softened the thread with the saliva in our mouths, and flattened it when we pulled it out through our teeth. Then we aimed the thread for the upper end of the needle and hoped we could get that tiny thread through it on the first try. It was impossible.

"I'd rather look for the needle in a stack of hay," I told Grace. "That'd be easier." Even with a needle a little larger than the job required, I couldn't do it. It was hard for all of us but Miss Simm was extremely encouraging. By the end of that first class, only one of the girls was able to thread her needle. By the end of the next day, almost everybody was able to thread the needles, everybody, that is, except two. I was one of the two. I got so mad. Then the next day when I found out I was the only one who couldn't do it my frustration got the better of me. I took my needle over to the window and threw it out. Miss Simm couldn't see at all so she didn't know what I had done. Later as we left the room, I talked with some of the other girls. Lena Riggs, whose room was next to mine in the dormitory, was with me at that time. "Why don't you let me thread it for you?" she offered.

"How am I going to do that? You're two rows away. You think I can just ask the other girls to pass it along to you so you can thread it and pass back to me?" I was angry and irritable.

She ignored my sarcasm. "Miss Simm can't see either one of us. You just get up and walk it over to me, and let me thread it while you wait. Take your shoes off so she can't hear you and then quietly slip back into your seat."

Now I began to get interested so the next day I tried it. Always at the school the chairs were kept in an order so we could move about with trust that the path would be clear. The rows were very precise and straight. I was very interested in this plan.

"It might work. It's worth a try." I was ready for anything by this time.

The next day, when the time came to thread the needle, I unbuttoned my shoes quietly and slipped them off, as quickly as I could, and moved over to Lena's spot, two rows over and three chairs from the end chair. I was a quiet as a rabbit. I didn't say a word, just tapped her on the shoulder. She reached up to get my needle and thread, threaded it, and I went back to my seat.

Miss Simm made such a fuss over me when she thought I had finally learned to thread the needle. She complimented me for my "determination." I hadn't thought about the guilty feeling I got when Miss Simm made over me for finally threading it. I said nothing.

"You see, students, what perseverance accomplishes?" she said.

I felt worse yet. Grace said later that she was tickled at Miss Simm's ill-founded compliments. She went on and on. "You'll always face difficult tasks, girls. Dive into the challenge head first, with determination and the conviction of your ability. You'll be surprised about what you can do. And so will others." Grace snickered.

Every day, Lena threaded my needle. That went on for several days. One day on the way out, Marla Richie said to me. "How come you can't thread your own needle? All the rest of us do. You have to, too."

"Oh, but I've tried and I can't do it," I complained.

"Sure you can't do it. That's because you don't try. You're a quitter, Ruth. Sure you can't do it, Ruth Christensen. You let somebody else do it for you and then took credit for doing it yourself. I think you're just lazy," she flashed accusingly.

"I'm not lazy. I can't do it," I argued, knowing I could go on forever with Lena, or somebody like her, threading it for me.

The next day, when sewing class started, I again quietly charged through the aisle in my stocking feet and headed around through the familiar route. Just before I got to Lena I ran straight into a chair in the middle of the aisle. I kicked the chair leg hard with my shin and sprawled down over the chair as it fell backward. "Ouch, my leg. Ou-h-h-h," I moaned.

Most of the girls knew it was going to happen. They planned it all. Marla pulled a chair out into the aisle before she sat down for class. Of course, when I fell, Miss Simm demanded to know what had happened. "What's going on. Who fell?"

The room fell silent. Again, her voice rose as she insisted on answers. I felt guilty, demoralized and low down. Besides my leg hurt and I bumped my head. The humiliation of her finding out what I had done was worse that the pain of my bruises.

"Me," I said. "Ruth. Ruth Christensen."

"What are you doing walking around the room, Ruth?"

"I can't thread my needle. I'm sorry."

"Who is threading your needle. Who has been threading your needle all along?" her voice rising as she demanded an answer.

I realized that I was about to get Lena in trouble, too, so said nothing else.

"Well," Miss Simm spoke. "Isn't this a fine pot of stew? You are a cheat, Miss Ruth Christensen. How do you feel about that? Aren't you ashamed of yourself?"

"Yes, mam. I'm sorry," I mumbled.

"Speak up. I can't hear you. What did you say?" she almost yelled.

"I'm sorry."

"Well, it's a little late to be sorry. I'll tell you what we're going to do with you, young lady. You can take your class out in the corner of the hall. You're going to stay there for every day this class is in session until YOU decide to thread your own needle. When you do that you can return to this class."

I began to cry. I really did feel sorry. Everyone thought I was a bad person.

"That'll do you no good at all." Miss Simm's anger at the deception caused her voice to almost yell. "You decide what you can do and what you don't WANT to do. It's not that you CAN'T do it. It's that you don't want to. And that's not the way we work around here."

I was already out into the hall. Frankly, I was glad to get out of there, away from the source of my humiliation. I left the room for the corner of the hall, still whimpering. The bell for the end of class rang in only about ten minutes, so I walked by myself to the conservatory where I could be alone. I went into one of the practice rooms and soon became lost in my music. That was my first choice, anyway, the place where I could always go when I wanted to be alone.

The next day, when sewing class time came again, I went directly to the corner of the hall. Miss Simm came out but just to ask if I was there. She was a tough teacher. But I knew I was wrong and I deserved the punishment. Within 15 minutes in the corner, I walked back into the sewing class and handed Miss Simm my threaded needle.

"No more tricks, Ruth. Did you actually thread this one yourself?" she asked suspiciously.

"Yes. I threaded it myself," I said rather defiantly. Was she always going to doubt me?

"Well, let's see you repeat that little chore," Miss Simm challenged. She was still burning from the earlier trick, as she yanked the thread from the needle and handed both the needle and thread back to me. "Here. Show me." It took a little time, but I did it. With that proof, I was able to join the class again. Even though I initially was mad at the girls for tricking me, by this time I'd begun to think that I had really deserved it. I held no grudges. By the time I heard Marla Richie's voice in the dining room at dinner, I was over it. I could now thread a needle. Just like everyone else, I could thread my own needle.

"I deserved it, Marla. I should have been caught. You were right. I could do it when I really tried."

*   *   *

American jazz and blues music was beginning to surface in the country. The school trained their students in serious, classical music and the Professor felt adherence to the strict and precise music was absolutely necessary for a proper background. In band, there was some occasions to play other kinds of music than the great marches of the day. But swing and other more informal type of music was "too sloppy" and "temporary" for us to "waste our time on" according to the Professor. Once or twice someone slurred his trumpet and the Professor scolded.

"Forget that music. You're going to have to make a living someday and you'll never be able to live on that," he'd say. However, he did allow a compromise with "Alexander's Ragtime Band" which was very popular at the time. He only tolerated it, acting as though he didn't hear it. He heard. It was his way of encouraging the search for new sounds in the music his students were writing. The Professor tried to be open about new rhythms and sounds without compromising his standards. It was only the senior students whom he permitted some relaxation on this policy.

Most of our teachers were pretty strict, some much more than others. The strictest, the nastiest, the loudest of all our teachers was Miss Backer, whom we assigned the name of "the Black Widow." She scolded or complained about something every time we were around her. One day, we got one of the girls who could see a little bit, Ida Collins, to lie in wait for her on the second floor landing. When The Black Widow walked under the landing, Ida poured this stinky perfume on her head. Oh, did she get mad? She thought we all had done it and yelled at everyone around. And there were a lot of girls within ear shot who laughed at the trick, even before they knew what we really did. When they heard her voice, they figured someone had finally gotten back at her, something everyone really wanted to do themselves. The Black Widow was right. We all wanted to do it so I guess we were all guilty.

Another day, when the Black Widow happened to be walking in the hall outside the chapel, Grace was practicing on the organ. For just a short minute, that particular minute when the Black Widow passed in front of the door, Grace was trying out "Alexander's Ragtime Band" on the organ.

The Black Widow swung the door open wide and yelled in an angry voice. "What do you think you are doing? Where's your respect for the church?"

Grace stopped playing. "I think it sounds better on the organ than the piano," she said in a very quiet voice. "It's not my fault the only organ in the school is in the Chapel."

"That has nothing to do with it," The Black Widow screamed. "This is a holy place and not a place to be disgraced with such trash."

"It's not trash," said Grace

"Silence," she bellowed. "Come with me right this minute. We're going to the superintendent's office and you, young lady, will go to detention."

Well, Grace was punished for the infraction and even though her feelings were bruised knew she had a good point. "There is no wrong music. God hears all voices and accepts all gifts of his people. Chapel or church is a safe place for new expressions, the kind of musical experiences intended to be only good."

We all agreed. In a little while the room fell silent. Grace spoke first.

"I think it's time we paid her back and make our own statement about the music in the Chapel."

"Have anything in mind?" Alice asked.

"Yes, I have. None of you like that old battle-ax, right?" We all agreed.

"Then I have a plan," Grace sounded mysterious. "Maude, can you find out when the next early morning time is that the Black Widow has duty on the Chapel floor?"

Ten minutes later, the plot had been completely set, with all five of us girls participating. It was to take place on the following morning, at five a.m. That was a full hour before wake up time was sounded. Everyone would still be asleep. Everyone, that is, except the night watchman. Maude had found out that at that hour he'd be making his rounds on the outside of the building. He wouldn't be a problem.

Maude played the trumpet, Alice the clarinet, and Tina the trombone. They were so excited to participate in hatching our plan that Grace woke us up just as the old roosters crowed at five o'clock the next morning. It was almost as though we had never been to sleep because we were so alert when the time came. I headed next door to wake up our neighbors, then in the other direction to get Tina moving. Her roommate woke up just as Tina was just getting up.

"What's going on?" she asked, with a yawn.

"We're out to give the Black Widow a piece of our minds. 'You want to come, too?" I asked.

"Sure. What can I do?"

"That's great. Can you sneak into the band room and get your snare-drums?" I giggled with expectation.

Thoughtfully, "I should be able to. What time is it now?"

Within six minutes she was back. They were all in my room, whispering. Adrenaline was running hard as all our excitement grew.

"Okay, let's go," I said.

"Follow me," Grace headed out "and remember no talking and be sure to stay up against the wall," as we headed downstairs.

All was quiet out in the hall. Gingerly, we glided over to the banister, across to the wall at the side of the steps, and almost floated down to the first floor. All's well. Everyone was asleep. We almost tipped our hand when we passed the open room of the Black Widow and doubled up into suppressed, but hysterical giggles at the snorting and snoring coming from inside.

"Her motor's turned on," I whispered.

"Yeah, and it's got air in the line. It'll sputter to a stop real soon," Grace quipped. We all snickered through our cupped hands.

We got to the Chapel door and quietly and slowly opened it. There was a very gentle squeak, enough to surprise and frighten us but apparently not enough to awaken anyone.

The girls filed inside and our rear guard closed the door behind them. I went to the Steinway grand piano, opened it and propped up the lid to its highest position. I wanted all the sound I could get from that piano, knowing fully what noise I had to compete with. I sat, centering my body on the bench, my back straight in full attention.

Grace glided right over to the organ and turned on the motor-switch. I could hear her as she dumped her girth onto the organ bench and swung her legs around under the manuals. I knew her right foot was searching for the volume pedal. It clicked when she pressed it down hard, into full position. She must not have noticed the smell of frying sausage drifting up from the kitchen, an odor that under any other circumstances would have captivated her attention.

The other girls took their places, spaced about the room as we had planned. They could move in a circular fashion for our "parade." They had paced off their route the day before, Tina down the center isle, Angela to the right, Maude to the left. The plan was to move up the outer sides, around the back meeting again in the center for the march down the center isle.

Alice stood at the door, waiting for Grace's signal. She shook with excitement.

"Okay," Grace whispered. "Everyone ready?"

"Let's go," Ruth said.

"Yeah," said Maude.

"One, two, three, go."

Alice threw open the Chapel door into the hall of the school, the snare drums broke out in a solid roll and the march was on, with organ, piano, trombone, trumpet, clarinet, and drums in the swingingest, jazziest and loudest version of Alexander's Ragtime Band that anyone ever heard. No one and No-body slept through the racket coming out of the Chapel that morning.

I cherished the though that the Black Widow was in a sound sleep and at the sound of the music, jerking to an upright position, at first believing she must be in a dream, blinking her eyes, shaking her head in disbelief. Then quickly swinging her legs out and her feet to the floor, groping for her bathrobe and slippers at the same time. Her hair must have been tousled and ragged. I understand she was still tying the belt of her robe as she entered the hall and began to trot down to the source of the noise.

Everyone at the school had to be awake also, and either moving toward the door or sitting straight up in bed to hear anything to help explain the commotion. I was later told, they realized it was too early for organized school and quickly grasped the situation. What bravery! They were tickled at the daring act.

When the Black Widow reached the chapel door, she shouted. "Stop this. Stop this, right this minute."

But nobody in the Chapel that morning had the sleep washed out of their ears yet, so we played on, swinging and swaying. I was told Tina's body arched when she played her trombone, and I figured Alice's body bounced from side to side timed to the beat and her music became more spirited as she swung through and around the pews. The snares gave the beat of a full marching band.

"Do you hear me?" She yelled. "I said to stop this, this very minute."

I could hear Grace giggling. And I realized that I was grinning from ear to ear, overjoyed in the greatest act of deserved defiance ever displayed in our young lives. For a full minute, we ignored the Black

Widow, until she got all the way down past the pews to the organ. She flipped off the organ switch.

The chapel fell silent, slowly into a deathly quiet. Not a breath could be heard. The terrible conspirators stayed in place, grinning with pleasure and so tickled with untold satisfaction.

"Well-l-l, just who do you think you are?" she demanded.

I got pretty sassy and disrespectful. "Grace, don't you have any education? Did I hear you say who instead of whom? Tut-tut."

"Twasn't me," Grace rolled back her head laughing. "I know better."

"Out! Out of here," the Black Widow screamed. "Straight to the superintendent's office."

"What for?" Maude said quietly. "Nobody's in there yet.

Every door to the upstairs rooms had opened and the students were out against the banisters to try to recognize the voices from below, the voices of the great ones who had put down the school's most disliked teacher. They cheered and laughed as our little group of musicians reached the stairway. I think at that moment the Black Widow realized she was beaten and for a split second, I felt a little sorry for her.

The superintendent had also been awakened in his house on campus but some distance away. He had come to investigate the commotion, himself, but he just stood in the distance down the hall and observed. Strangely, he didn't seem offended by it. As a matter-of-fact, Grace said she thought he rather enjoyed our daring.

He sent us all, including Miss Backer, to our rooms to get dressed and ready for Chapel, with instructions to come to his office immediately following Chapel. We knew we were in trouble, probably big trouble, but his attitude about it was really surprising to us all. He kind of chuckled when he talked with us. He just put us all on detention. But nothing dampened our personal satisfaction in the parade of the chapel. And we were heroes to the whole school.

Men's gymnastic team at Arkansas Scholl for the Blind

Arkansas School for the Blind in 1900, Little Rock, Arkansas

Ruth with new washing machine, circa 1920's

Christensen family–Front row, Mary, Ruth, Peter.
Back row–Anna, Esther, Inger.

CHAPTER ELEVEN

Professor Trebing

Professor Trebing had come to the school from a very successful teaching position in Kentucky and was well established as a composer of note in his own right, and a fine composition coach. His reputation was so prestigious that of all the teachers at the school he was the only one earning that greatest of respect by being labeled with The Professor. All other teachers were Mr. or Miss whoever but The Professor could only be Professor Trebing. He came in an instructor-team with his wife. The professor was completely blind and his wife had full sight. His responsibilities were as music department head and to teach piano, organ and band. To the advanced students he also taught music composition.

Mrs. Trebing had a lovely soprano voice and was in demand around the state as a lyric soprano soloist. Her position at the school required her to teach voice, choir and glee clubs, harmony and to the most talented music students, beginning composition. An apartment on the school grounds was part of their salary arrangement.

We parents were told very early that preparing blind children for a career as a professional musician, whether it be as an orchestra saxophonist or church organist, made the music department one of the most important departments at the school. A child with average of better intelligence, a good sense of rhythm and musical aptitude was a good candidate for extensive training in that department. Every effort was made to tap the latent talents and to cultivate abilities as they were recognized. The primary goal of the school was to prepare each student to ultimately make one's own living, independent of family and friends.

Of course, it was impossible for these students to see a score of music to play by. They had to memorize every piece of music they played. Both Braille and a newer system, called New York Point, were forms used for blind music students. A student of piano, for instance, read his music with his left hand as he played with his right hand. Again and again, he played it. He repeated that process to learn the left hand. Then the two hands, now in his or her memory, were put together. Expression and musical color, or expression and volume, were added. The same process was used for the instruments. So the method was repetitive and tedious, boringly tedious.

Other ways of learning were for those who had perfect pitch and excelled in musicology, that is, intuitively knew rhymes, harmonies and chord structures could memorize by simply listening to another play.

The Professor was an out and out favorite of his students. He was a master at motivation, most of the time in a subtle and gentle way. On occasion, he became a little manipulative, but they responded to him. His patience and encouragement were as much a part of him as his mustache or his nose. He was never without any of them. When Ruth balked at working so hard, he would say.

"Child, if you really don't want to work today, you don't have too. But you must remember you must make it up tomorrow. You'll have to work twice as hard and twice as long. That's a long time. Is that what you want to do?"

She began to think about how badly she really wanted to lag off. Then, he'd let her make the choice.

"Do you really think you want to work that long tomorrow? It's all up to you. Now, you tell me what you want to do?"

Well, ninety-nine times out of one hundred the student decided to continue. Ruth always did. He made her think about it and she knew she had a choice.

Music students practiced four hours a day. Students in the Industrial

Arts Department worked to produce a product. Musicians were also working to produce a product, a different kind of product.

By the time a student in Industrial Arts graduated from school he or she knew how to make a mattress well enough to be hired for that purpose. The same applied to weaving a rug, making a broom, or playing the trumpet or pipe organ. So each day was filled from 6 a.m. to 8 p.m., including the three meals served in the school dining room, or course.

Most music students studied more than one instrument. Even if they had no aptitude for music, they were at least given a try to be sure a hidden musical talent wasn't to be developed. A violinist also learned how to play the other strings, viola, cello and bass. Keyboard players would play the piano and organ, or the piano and a string or wind instrument, and maybe a xylophone, Celeste, chimes or drum. Most of the music students were also in one of the singing groups, glee club, senior or junior choir and if any talent exposed itself, the student began to write music, to compose. With so much activity in each semester, there was only time for one private lesson per week in any given instrument.

Living together and working such long days provided them social activities as well as their learning and training. This was home. For the most part, they became like brothers and sisters and took a strong interest in each other, even including some normal sibling rivalry. It was understood that the greatest opportunity for learning occurred when the students enjoyed the whole atmosphere, and they did with the exception of the infamous Black Widow. The Professor was so effective because he knew exactly the right thing to say to bring out the best in each of his charges. He teased, he threatened, he loved and encouraged humor, both spoken and in the works they performed.

The opportunities to chat and gossips were numerous. It seemed to the older girls that the Professor used a different tone of voice when he spoke to Lillian Pullum. There was a sexiness in her voice when talking to him and he responded with a soft and almost salacious tone. The girls picked up on this. They all talked about the Professor being 'sweet on Lillian Pullum.' Maude said one day that she was sure something was going on. "Nobody talks to the Professor like she has molasses in her mouth, that is, nobody except Lillian." Maude said, "I intend to find out what is going on."

"How're you going to do that?" Ruth asked.

"I'm going to listen at the door when Lillian has her piano lesson."

"Oh, what can you hear from that?" Ruth pressed.

"Well, nothing if anyone's coming down the hall. But then, I don't want to be caught sneaking around listening at the door, either."

"Well," Ruth began to think about it. "Why don't we listen outside?"

"What can we hear outside with all the noise out there?" There was doubt in Maude's voice.

After thinking a bit, Ruth answered. "We can crawl behind the bushes so we'll be close to the building and just under the windows. We'll listen just outside. They can't close the windows this time of year and no one can see us down behind the bushes."

"What'd you mean WE?" demanded Tina.

"I wanta be there," proclaimed Ruth.

"Not without me." chipped in Grace.

Ruth took over. "Okay, okay, we'll all go. Let's see, when does Lillian have her next lesson? Anybody know?"

"She's in just before mine," Grace announced. "That'll be tomorrow at three o'clock."

"Okay, meet at the door on the south side, closest to the practice rooms, at ten minutes 'til three."

"Wow! Whata 'ya thinks goin on?"

"I think they're playing WHOOPEE."

Everyone giggled. "Oh, wouldn't that be just the wildest thing this school has ever known?" someone said.

"Yeah. I can't wait."

Maude began, "Apple, peaches, creamery butter," in a sing-song manner.

And the others joined in, smiling and giggling.

> *What's the name of my true lover?*
> *"We shall see, we shall see,"* they squealed.

"Tomorrow, we shall see,.
Remember, ten til three."

"Gotta go," someone called out.

They all went their own way, each one excited with the anticipation of the discovery coming up tomorrow.

Ruth walked away with Grace toward the practice rooms, giggling with anticipation, and quietly talking about their secret sleuthing.

"Grace," called out by a low, male voice from behind.

The girls stopped and turned to face the voice. "Someone call me?"

"Yeah! I called you."

By this time Grace recognized the voice. "Oh, Hello, John." (It was John McCracken.)

"Hello, John," Ruth acknowledged.

"What's goin' on?" John returned.

"Oh, we're goin' over to the conservatory. Grace is headin' for the Chapel to prac . . ."

"No, that's not what I mean," John interrupted. "You girls are cookin' up some trouble, aren't you?"

"What ever do you mean, John McCracken?" Grace began with her most timid and bashful voice.

"Don't give me that innocent pitch," John challenged. "That won't work with this ol' boy. Come on, give."

"You're just suspicious, John." Ruth chipped in.

"Yeah, John! Your suspicion is really unfounded in fact." And changing the subject to put an end to the questions, Grace said. "I hear you're getting ready for the All State Competition next week. I heard you dragging your magnificent basso through OLD MAN RIVER. You're certain to win with that, John. IT IS beautiful!"

"Well-l. Thanks. I didn't even know you knew I was singing solo. But that number is one of my favorites. I love singing it."

"Here we are already at the practice room, John" Ruth said

Grace offered, "We'll see you later, John."

"See ya', girls." As he walked away he considered the clever way they changed the subject. Ah, ha. No matter, though. I got the time and the place . . . hum,m,m."

John was one of the students who had some sight. He turned to look back at them through his thick glasses, but they were already out of his sight. "Through the doors, already," he said to himself. "Nice girls, really."

Ruth sat at the piano bench, with the Professor pacing the floor around the room. "Color. Color, Child. You play in black and white, today. What's the matter? The music should not be just bright or dark. It's all colors of the rainbow, happy music, maybe a little rain, but not just dull overcast or blizzard condition. Isn't your mind on your piano lesson, yah?"

"Let me start again," Ruth offered. "I need to get my breath before beginning."

"Wise thinking, Child. Take a walk around the piano. Take a deep breath. Raise your shoulders up, up, up to your ears. Roll 'em back, slow-ow-ly, inhale deeply, relax and let out all the air from your lungs. Push it all out and breathe deeply again," he said in his thick German accent.

"Now, come back to the piano. Start again. Think about what you are playing. Play it with velvet fingers. Imagine you are wearing velvet gloves. Legato, child. Lazy legato."

By the time the lesson was over, the supper cooking odors were already drifting up to the hallway, and Ruth was starved. The suppertime bell sounded and the rush of hungry students heading to the dining room was a little like a buffalo stampede.

"I've never heard a buffalo stampede," Ruth said to herself, "but I think it wouldn't sound any quieter."

"I think it's pork for tonight. 'Wonder what it is? Pork-chops, maybe. If it's roast pork or chops, we'll still get mashed potatoes and gravy. And probably biscuits, too. Buttermilk biscuits. Um-m-m, good. I can't wait."

She could hear Grace's voice in the distance. "I need to satisfy my enormous carnal appetite with exuberance and full appreciation."

She always said that. Ruth grinned when she heard it. "I know why she's so fat. She always asks for seconds. And she eats like she hasn't eaten anything for a week. Everyday, it's like this."

"Hi, Ruth." It was John McCracken's voice. "Have you met Homer Hudlow?"

"No." Her head was slightly downward, as if watching the ground in front of her feet. "Howdy, Homer," face half turned toward John's voice, just as she was taught. Of course, it was only a guess, where Homer was, but since John was on that side, it was likely his friend was with him.

She was right. The unfamiliar voice answered. "Hello, Ruth. Mind if we eat with you girls tonight?"

"Fine. Fine. 'Glad to have your company. That's for sure." Ruth answered. "It sounds like your voice is coming from way up there, Homer. Just how tall are you. Homer?"

John picked up on that immediately. "He's so tall and skinny, we call him BEAN-POLE," John laughed.

Grace picked up the voices she was interested in from several feet away and gradually, moved over closer, following the sounds of their voices to guide her.

"Who's a bean-pole?" she interjected.

The boys sat directly across the table from the girls this evening. It was an interesting and very funny conversation.

"Aren't they nice?" Ruth asked later.

"Yeah," Grace answered. "Aren't they funny?"

*   *   *

At ten minutes 'til three the next day, the girls were at the door as planned Little did they know, so were the boys. But the boys stayed out of earshot and John waited until they moved out of the building to begin his tracking.

The girls walked down the steps, following the wooden banister down to the brick and concrete pillar next to the bottom step. Ruth spoke first.

"We have to pace off the distance to the end of the building 'cause they'll be in the corner room. The bushes are too thick there so we'll have to come back and move in to the base of the building right where the steps end."

"Silly," Grace argued. "Why pace it off. We can just follow the wall to the outside corner."

"Yeah, but we have to be careful to get around the basement windows. The concrete around them sticks out. Some one might fall down in one of them."

"Let me lead," Ruth suggested. "I know just how wide those windows are. Follow me."

Ruth headed into the bushes along side the steps leading up to the building, lightly touching the base of the under-structure for guidance. She was trailed by Grace, Maude and Sally, in that order. After making the 90 degree turn onto the long wall, she slowly, carefully, glided forward, left arm on the building as she lead with her right foot, sweeping her toe in a wide swath to find the obstructions around the basement windows. As she came to them, one by one, she turned to explain it to Grace in a quiet manner.

"Ouch," Maude popped out.

"Shush-h-h!" Grace turned around. In a loud, scolding whisper, "Quiet! Be quiet, you two."

In the rear, Sally gently said, "What's the matter?"

"Oh, it's just these darn branches. They stuck me in the arm. It hurt."

Grace's head turned back just slightly. "We'll get caught, if you keep that up. Can't you just wait to complain 'til we're outta here?"

Ruth stopped. "Wait." She listened for sounds above.

"Why're we stopping? Are we under his window?" Pause before Sally again said. "Somebody answer me."

Ruth's irritation showed, "How can I hear with all the blabbering coming from the rear? Be quiet so I can hear."

Then she heard it, that giddy, silly giggle of Lillian Pullum. Ruth grinned. "That's Lillian. Listen to her giggle."

They each snickered, trying to hold it in either their sleeve or a cupped hand. Then for the first time they heard the Professor, with a lilting voice.

"Now, dear child. Play that again, this time think about vhat you are trying to convey in this music. It's not a love song, you know. You play it like it vas a love song, rather like syrup or honey. Tell me. Vhat is the story here?"

Giggling like the immature 16 year old she was, Lillian's voice came between giggles. "Why, professor, I didn't expect you here on the bench with me."

Ruth turned. "Did you hear that? He's sitting on the piano bench with her. He never sits with me."

"Me, neither," Sally pushed in.

"What's he doing now?" Maude demanded.

"Sh-h-h."

"Give me your hand, Child. It's so nice and warm. Are you nervous, my dear?"

"He's holding her hand."

"Golly, gosh."

"What's next?" A deep male voice boomed out within two or three feet of them. Homer and John had followed them on the outside of the bushes and were also listening to the conversation in the upstairs window.

"Those girls. My, my, what DO you think they're up to?"

All four were completely silenced, hoping they were not the ones to which the reference was being made.

"Do you mean Ruth and Grace? Yes? And I believe Maude and uh . . . is that Sally with them?

The jig was up. The girls scrambled out on their stomachs, until it appeared they were clear of the landscaping around the building. Grace was struggling to her feet.

"Do you need my most courteous and chivalrous assistance, Miss Davenport?"

Ruth charged. "What are you doing here?"

"I could ask you the same thing, Miss Christensen."

Sally said. "You followed us, didn't you?"

"Well-l-l, perhaps we are bloodhounds. You can just call us the Braille Bloodhounds," said Homer.

"You left a trail of noise similar to a stream of angry bees. But truthfully, we've been right behind you from the beginning." John chuckled.

"Hey, it was just getting good," Sally whined.

"That's okay," Maude rationalized. "Now we know for sure the Professor is sweet on Lillian Pullum."

"Yeah, we found out all we needed to know," Sally said.

"Come on, girls, you don't KNOW anything. You're just building up a scene in your own minds. Forget it, girls. You've had your fun." Homer broke in. "Now, how'd you like to play a trick on our favorite professor?"

"A trick? What kind of trick?"

"Whatta' you got in mind, Homer?"

"Well, meet us tomorrow about this same time and we'll tell you our plan."

"Oh, tell us now. What are you going to do?"

"Now, now, ladies. Don't push. Tomorrow, same time, same place."

Their voices trailed as they walked away.

CHAPTER TWELVE

The Professor's Car

The next day in Geometry class, Mr. Mason, the instructor, asked if anyone in the room would care to give the equation for determining the total volume of a 50 foot cylinder which was 18 feet in diameter. The responding student was not acknowledged by name but I recognized the voice. It was a surprise to find out that I had a class with Homer Hudlow.

I listened to the self confidence in his voice. It was a deep voice, too. "I wonder if the feelings are deep, too," I smiled to myself, as I listened to the rise and fall of his voice.

"I wonder what he looks like. I'll bet he sings, also. The timber of his voice and the resonance means he's already trained or I'll bet the Professor is turning handsprings to get him into advanced choir."

When the class was over, I poked around in picking up my things before leaving the room. My ploy was to talk with Homer and it worked for he had already found out where I sat and walked over to my desk. I could sense someone standing right in front of me as he spoke.

"Hello again, Ruth. How's the detective today?"

I threw back my head as I laughed. "A little scratched and bruised, but none the worse for the experience."

"I'm heading up to the conservatory. Where're you going?" he asked. "I'm on the schedule for organ practice in the Chapel," I answered.

He began, "We're going right b . . ." His sentence was interrupted by the loud ringing of the fire alarm. Three two-second rings, one off, and three more rings, again and again. It continued. My attention was fixed on the bells.

"Sounds serious," I told him. "Have you been here long enough to know the fire drill rules."

"I'm afraid not."

"Never mind, I'll help you. Give me your hand."

Mr. Mason's voice punctured the air. "Order. Order, here. It's probably just a drill. You all know what to do. Form a double line, hold hands and file out. Move like it was a real fire."

I felt Homer take my hand. "Come with me," I told him as I pulled him out the door in a fast moving pace. We stayed close to the wall on the right side of the hall until we rounded the corner just in front of the fire escape.

"It's great fun," I explained. "I love the fire drills and a chance for a good slide."

"What'd you mean?" Homer asked.

"It's a big, three story slide, and let me tell you, it moves you down fast. You'll have to catch your breath. By that time, you're already on the ground. Follow me."

I dropped his hand as I sat on the edge of the giant metal slide contained inside a great mesh, cylinder. I quickly swung my legs around and with a little scoot I was on my way. "Sit down and just push yourself off." My voice trailed as I sailed down to the ground.

"Ger-ate!" I heard him right behind as I scrambled out of his way. I knew to move away fast or get kicked in the butt so I scrambled over to the side. Homer quickly picked himself up as he caught up with me. He grabbed my hand. "*He can see.*" I thought to myself. "*There's no way he could find my hand so fast unless he can see.*" I started to laugh.

"Why are you laughing?" he asked.

"Because, here I am, a blind girl making my way out through the fire and thick smoke, leading you out, saving you from a terrible fire, you with two good eyes?"

"What makes you think I can see?" he teased.

"Everybody sees here," I flashed.

"I mean, how do you know I can SEE anything?"

"Silly, you found me. And quickly. That is you're quicker than a person following the sound of a footstep or voice." I answered.

"I'm a country boy. My instincts are good," he answered.

"Maybe so, but not that good," I reasoned. "Tell me I'm right, Homer Hudlow," I coaxed.

"You are right, Miss Christensen," just then, apparently realizing he still held my hand, he dropped it.

"Oh, are we safe from the fire," I teased.

"There's no fire. I don't see any smoke," he offered.

"I know." I stood up, holding my oversized Braille book in one arm.

"How do you know?" He doubted me.

"Because I couldn't smell any smoke. Who ever heard of a fire without smoke. Maybe the other way around, smoke without a fire, but, believe me, if there was a fire I'd smell smoke."

"What if its too early for smoke?" he pushed.

"Then I'd still smell it. You can't miss that odor?"

The alarm bell sounded an all clear signal. He picked up my hand again. "Can I help you up?"

"Good manners," I thought to myself. Then aloud, I asked him, "How well do you see?"

"My tear ducts work all the time. My eyes water so much that I can't focus well so I can see some but not clearly. Otherwise, there's nothing wrong with my eyes."

"And you're in this school?" I questioned.

"I believe they're going to operate on my eyes and remove my eye-lashes. I had an accident, you see, back home on the farm. My eye lashes permanently turn inward and scratch the eyeball. Naturally, the tears rush out to wash off those scratchy lashes. Only, the lashes don't leave. They're there permanently."

"Oh, I see!" I understood.

We both laughed. By this time we had reached the door into the Chapel. "This is your stop. Thanks for saving me from the fire." he laughed. "I'll see you later."

"Anytime. Look me up the next fire you're in. I'm happy to save a fellow student. See you later," I repeated. "Tomorrow at ten minutes till three."

"Before that, I hope," he said.

I walked away smiling. My step was light and spirited as I walked down the aisle to the organ. I felt good.

* * *

The next day John was waiting in the hallway as Grace and I walked up. We got quiet so we could hear the boy's voices before we got to the meeting place. Homer was just behind John, a little more distant but I was able to pick up his voice.

Just as we gave our "Hellos" Sally and Maude rushed up, anxious to be included in the secret activity, whatever it was.

"We miss anything?" Sally questioned.

"Not a thing," Homer said. "We just got here, too."

"What's going on?" I was anxious.

"Yeah, tell us," Grace begged.

"Let's go outside so nobody can hear us," John's voice trailed out the door.

One-by-one, we all filed out, down the lawn to a safe distance from the building.

"Where're we going?" someone asked.

John stopped and turned around to face the others.

"You know the Professor has a new car," he began. "It a nice, new car."

"Yeah. I heard." I said.

"No, I didn't know," Sally offered.

"Well it really doesn't matter that you knew it before or not. The point is that he parks it in a garage around at the front of the school, on Eighteenth Street. We had all ears on him.

"So?" Grace's voice was a little annoyed. He continued. "Would you like to play a trick on the Professor, a trick with his car? You know, so he can't back it out of the garage."

Grace spoke up quickly. "I'm not into damaging his car. That's not the way I like to play."

She was interrupted by John McCormick. "You don't understand. There's not going to be any damage to the car or the garage. We're simply going to turn the car around inside the garage. You know, so it's in there sideways and he can't back it out."

"You can't do that. At least, I don't think you can. Have you tried it?" I asked.

"No, but we think we can do it," Homer answered.

"Well, let's make sure it can be done first. Why don't we make a model, of the exact proportions of both the car and the garage. Then we can see if it can be turned inside that garage. I think in the least, you might bend a fender or scratch his car and that wouldn't be very nice. I like the Professor, he's one of my favor . . ." I was interrupted by Homer.

"You still don't understand. We'll get some of the other boys and lift it to move it. We can turn it inside the garage."

"My swannee! How much does it weigh?" I asked.

"I'm not sure, but it's not that heavy. When you look at the size of the axle, and the frame is wooden, it doesn't look like it weighs that much," Homer explained.

"Well, let's get the actual dimensions and check out if it can be turned at all," I said. "Can you boys get a yard stick in the Manual Arts Department. Two of you can get into the garage and do the measurement. Is it locked?"

"I've already checked that," John answered. "I know its not locked and yes, I can borrow a measuring tool. Come on, Homer, let's go."

"Wait a minute," I said. "Girls, let's get some paper, the heavy kind we use in our Braille slate, and we'll use that for our models. John and Homer, meet us in the library in 30 minutes."

We got to the library first, and were not there long before we discovered that nasty old lady, Miss Arbuckle, was substituting. "What an old crabapple, she is!" Sally described her accurately. She'd be right on us and want to know what we were doing and why we were doing it. So by the time the boys got there with the measurement, we decided that the boys would make the car to scale and we girls would cut the paper for the garage. We'd have to separate ourselves from them in the library to avoid Miss Arbuckle's nosey curiosity. When we both have folded the paper to size, we can come back outside to this spot for the test. Everyone agreed. In 15 minutes we got down to the outer lawn where the boys were already waiting.

"Nobody can hear us here," John said. It would fit. With a foot to spare, we could pick up the car and turn it.

"With enough help, it can be done," Homer said. "Let's see, John, let's get four more fellows, three at each bumper. That should be enough. Now, when shall we do it?"

John spoke, "Let's pull it off tomorrow. Meet us down at the garage, at three thirty. You girls can't do anything."

I said, "Hey, don't leave us out of the fun. We'll be there for the spirit of the team."

Sure enough, when we got to the garage just after three thirty the next afternoon, there were four other male students inside when we got there.

We girls did no lifting but were thrilled to be included in the trickery. We stayed back just outside the door when the men began to work on the car. John took command. He called out his orders.

"Okay, men. One hand is on the wall to get your bearings. The other is on the bumper. We're going to synchronize our motion. We'll move by rhythm by bouncing the car on its springs. Two bounces. On the third, we pick it up together and move counter-clockwise to the forth count."

"Can't be done," someone called out.

"Sure, it can. It's going to be tight but Homer and I already have figured it out. It'll work."

There was a rumble of conversation in the garage and John ordered it quiet so they could proceed. "ONE, TWO, PICK IT UP, and MOVE. Take a breath. One, two, pick it up and move." Everyone paused, waiting for further instructions.

"Stand tall, men and relax for a count of four. And then go at it again. One, two, lift and move. You're doing great. We're almost to the corner. Now again."

That went on for several minutes. We girls were excited about the stunt and stayed quiet so we could hear the action inside the garage. When they had finished, they opened the doors and invited us in. We got to go over and take a look for ourselves. There was only one door and we'd come in it. We walked straight in, and right into the car door, that is, the side of the car. The front and rear bumpers were lined up with the side walls. It was the darnest thing.

"How'll he ever back it out?" Grace inquired.

"With considerable difficulty," John popped out quickly and we all laughed.

We knew the Professor was going to a meeting of the competition committee down town. It was to be a four thirty meeting. John checked the watch in his pocket, pulled it out and pressed the lid open. He touched the face of the watch to determine the position of the hour and minute hands on the dial.

"Hey, group! We better clear out while we can."

We walked around to the side of the garage away from the main school building. Homer was the only one who could see much of anything so he was our lookout. Shortly, he could see two figures coming closer, down the walk from the main building but he couldn't see well enough to identify them. He could only wait until they got close enough to hear them talking. It was the Professor and Mrs. Trebing.

"Hey, quiet. I think this is them."

The Trebings walked around to the front on Eighteenth Street, unlatched the simple slide lock and one by one, opened the doors of the garage.

With the first squeak of the garage door, the little group leaning against the side wall snickered and tried to smother our giggles. There was a little scream from Mrs. Trebing.

"Something wrong? What is it?" the Professor tilted his head, waiting for his wife to answer.

"Well, I'll swan!" She drawled in astonishment, trying to figure out how this happened. "I don't believe my eyes."

"What don't you believe?" the Professor demanded to know. "Tell me what's going on. What's inside the garage?"

"Emil, move forward and see for yourself."

The Professor was already edging over with curiosity so he needed no encouragement from his wife. He touched the car almost instantly. He expected the rear tire to be at the tips of his fingers as it would have been mounted on the back of his car. He didn't find the tire so he moved both hands, simultaneously, in an outward motion, following the line of the vehicle. His first thought was that the spare tire and wheel had been removed. But instead he found a door handle. A DOOR HANDLE.

"What the helephant's going on.?" almost to himself.

"I think we are the victims of someone's idea of humor," Mrs. Trebing explained. "You see, Emil, the car's in here but it's in sideways and I can't for the life of me, see how it got that way," she said incredulously. "And how're we going to get it out."

"Well, if someone got in it sideways, then someone can get it OUT," he rationalized and enunciated with an over-emphasis on the OUT."

The Trebings stayed and stayed. They couldn't believe this could happen. The Professor doubted what he was seeing but when he began to realize what had been done, "certainly by his students," he chuckled. He laughed. And he laughed some more.

"Halloween, is in just a few days," the Professor said. "I think we've been visited by the goblins a little early this year, some school goblins, no doubt," he chuckled.

"Oh, Emil, how can you take this so lightly. We can't get the car out of the garage. This is insulting."

"To the contrary, my dear. This is a compliment to us. If they weren't fond of us, do you think they'd waste their time. This is a statement of our esteem, of our importance to them. No harm's been done. And, if they got the car in this way, it can GET OUT the same way."

They both followed the walk back up to the school and in a few minutes were walking down the path again with the Superintendent and several other teachers. The group entered the garage and laughed as they examined the position of the car and pondered the brilliance of the move.

"Oh-h–" Hey, this is an engineering feat. Now, let me think a minute. Who would be clever enough to figure out how to do this. Hum-m-m," the Superintendent mumbled, quietly. "You're not saying much, all of a sudden, Trebing."

"Yes, I think I know who did it," he answered with a grin.

The Professor said nothing, not to any of his classes or to any of the students. But the next day, as John opened up one of the upright pianos in his piano mechanic's lab, he reached down inside to remove the action of the instrument.

There was a loud SNAP, he yelled and quickly withdrew, as he struggled to remove the mousetrap that was attached to his forefinger. As soon as the pressure was off the pinch, and he rubbed his compressed forefinger to renew the blood supply, he wondered it he'd been found out. Or was this just another student trick?

Actually, it happened again, not once but two more times. After that he reached down into the inside of the piano with his tuning hammer first to test the space. IF there had been another mousetrap the hammer would have activated it and saved his wounded fingers. There were no other traps.

Only the Superintendent had noticed a figure of a man standing across the street watching the activities around the garage that day. Other staff saw him but paid no attention. The Superintendent was alert to him. He wondered who he was, why he didn't seem to have anything to do, anyplace to go. Why was he there?

CHAPTER THIRTEEN

Fun and Talent

Students could stay in the dining room after the evening meal if we wanted to, as long as we were supervised. Some of us had to practice, study or do chores, but more and more, it seemed that a group of us stayed to enjoy each other's company after supper.

"Well," said Grace with her usual aplomb, "this has been a most sumptuous meal. I think it has satisfied my most carnal appetite with the greatest of exuberance."

"That's just saying you ate the vittles," Oscar Banks said from the other side of the table.

"No, Oscar. You're speaking Ozarkian. I'm speaking city-talk. It's a different language," Grace chided him, her head gently downcast and her ever-ready smile. Everyone laughed.

Homer sat down at the piano. His long legs angled awkwardly out to each side as he got close enough for his fingers to tickle the keys. He diddled a few lines, enough to get encouragement from the others in the room who then moved in closer to surround him. He ran through an introduction. This one's called Three Nights of Experience. He started to sing.

> *"The first night when I came home as drunk as I could be,*
> *I found a horse a standing in the stable where my horse orta be.*
> *So come in here me little wifie and explain this thing to me.*

*How come a horse is standing in the stable where my horse orta
be?*
*Ya blind fool, ya crazy fool, can't you ever see? 'Nothin but a
milk cow your granny sent to me.*
*I traveled this world over four thousand miles or more,
'Saddle upon a milk cow, I never did see before."*

We laughed our encouragement as one of the boys gave a muffled
war-hoop. Homer began his second verse.

*"The second night when I came home as drunk as I could
be,*
*I found a coat a hangin on the hanger where my coat orta
be.*
*So come in here me little wifie and explain this thing to me
How come a coat's a hangin on the hanger where my coat
orta be"*
Nothin but a bed quilt your granny sent to me.
*I've traveled this world over four thousand miles or more,
Pockets on a bed quilt, I never did see before."*

"Yeah, Homer, give us more." The supervising teacher in the room
at the time was a new lady, a very young person and much more
relaxed than our usually tough and aged old hens.
"Don't slow down now, Bean Pole," yelled a voice from the back.

"The third night when I came home as drunk as I could be,
I found a head a layin on the pillow where my head orta be.
So come in here me little wifie and explain this thing to me.
*How come a head's a layin on the pillar where my head orta
be?*
Ya blind fool, ya crazy fool, can't ya ever see
Nothin' but a cabbage head your granny sent to me.
*I've traveled this world over four thousand miles or more,
But a mustache on a cabbage head, I never did see before."*

We all clapped and tried not to make so much noise that another monitor, or house mother, might overrule the new, very patient lady.

Grace called out. "Get Ruth to sing her Old Maid's Song."

"Yes please do, Ruth."

"Come on Ruth, deliver your song at our feet."

Homer slid off the piano bench as I moved forward, tickled to death to be asked. I sat down, reaching from side to side of the keyboard to perfect my position in the center of the piano, and after running over an arpeggio, I began to sing. My song was peppier. I moved faster. And I sang it like a story of suspense and fright, with moments of almost whispering and other times of almost yelling. The group was completely quiet so as not to miss a word.

> *I'll sing you a song of a burglar bold, who tried to rob a house.*
> *He lifted the window* (I stretched up my shoulders and threw back my head as I dramatized the high note,) *and crept in, as quiet as a mouse."* (almost whispering.)
> *"He looked for a place to hide himself, til the folks were fast* (long hold) *asleep, he said I'll get their money, then take a quiet sneak."* (again very quietly, as the room listened, mesmerized.)
> *"And under the bed the burglar crept, he lay up close to the wall.*
> *He never knew 'twas an old maid's room or he's never have had the gall.*
> *But the clock struck nine and he saw a sight that made his hair turn gray.*
> *"At nine o'clock the old maid came in. 'Oh, I am so tired, she said.*
> *The burglar, he had seventeen fits as he looked from under the bed.*
> *She took out her teeth and her bum glass eye and the hair all off of her head."*

Everyone in the room seemed able to picture her bald head and toothless face. Almost every family had a relative with false teeth and they all removed them at night and dropped them in a cup or glass of soda water to soak overnight. Most of the kids in the room either had one or two glass eyes and laughing about themselves never upset any of them. They snickered and giggled, quietly so as not to miss any of my lines.

> *"From under the bed the burglar crept, he looked at the total wreck.*
> *The old maid, she was wide awake and she grabbed him by the neck.*
> *She never screamed or fainted a bit but was just as cool as a clam.*
> *She said 'my prayers are answered for at last I've found a man.*
> *The old maid drew a revolver and to the burglar said.*
> *'Young man, if you don't marry me, I'll blow off the top of your head.'*
> *The burglar looked at her bum glass eye and then at her awful"* (holding this note long and rolling my shoulders around my body) *"Snoot,*
> *He folded his arms across his chest and said, 'For God's sake, Shoot.,"*

I shouted, and gave a two note finale on the piano as the room broke apart.

John pulled out a harmonica and played "The Blue Tail Fly" and "Dixie." The head house mother came in and told us we should already be in our rooms. The "in bed" bell had already sounded, but none of us heard it. Slowly, we shuffled out, mingling and holding to every minute of this fun time.

"Goodnight, girls."

"Goodnight. See ya in the morning."

Homer was not in the dining room for breakfast. John said he wasn't feeling well. He missed all his classes that day and the following day, I heard that his fever was very high. Grace had heard he was put into quarantine in the dispensary.

His home was in the mountains in the upper part of the state. He was too sick to travel even if his folks could have come for him. So, he was placed in isolation, which was a separate building off to itself. It was the one area of the dispensary off limits to all the school except Miss Minnie, the school nurse.

Miss Minnie, was old enough to be Homer's mother, was tiny framed, only a little bigger "than a button", someone had once described. She was always cheery and pleasant. No one could remember a hard word ever coming out of her. And her patients were all just like her own children. Her tenderness with all of us was no different than our own mother's would have been. And that's what she did, not just in taking care of Homer but for the other three in the dispensary who came down with Scarlet Fever.

It was a disease to be feared. The permanent damage possible would have been caused by the fever. Getting and keeping it down was essential and Miss Minnie spent more than one thirty-six hour period, without sleep, dozing just occasionally, as she sat in her chair bathing his head, limbs and chest in the light mixture of tepid water and alcohol.

The entire mood of the school was reflected in the danger of death for any one or all of our Scarlet Fever patients. It was somber. School went on but clearly it was like a dark cloud had dropped onto the building, for there was no energy left, just apprehension and concern.

The school was family to all of us. It was where most of us stayed for twenty-four hours a day, for many months at a time. It was a family substitute with the real families miles away and without the financial means to travel in to the state capital for even a visit. Fellow students were brothers and sisters and teachers were parents, sometimes strict and disciplining and with others coaxing with subtlety and cleverness to lead their charges into our best.

On the morning of the third day, Miss Minnie, a very tired Miss Minnie, came out of her dispensary and went down to her housing.

Several hours later, she emerged, fresh and clean, with a smile of relief and success on her face. I'm sure she was still tired. She only napped a short while but she did rest. She burned all of her clothes when she took her bath, as well as all the other clothes in the dispensary. No one could accept an epidemic at the school so she was intent on protecting her charges as well as she knew how.

The immediate crisis was past, but shortly two others came down with scarlet fever. They all survived, each grateful forever to the loyal Miss Minnie who had loved and cared for them so tenderly. Grace and I remembered the fragrance of some wild flowers near the fence at the side of the school. We searched around to find them and picked some to leave at the door of the recovering patient.

* * *

Every year a major competition in piano performance was held for the entire state. It was always held on a Saturday at the high school in Little Rock. Any and all students enrolled in a public or private school in Arkansas could qualify as long as they abided by the competition rules. There was never any special consideration given for us because we were blind or had any physical limitation. As a matter had any assistance on stage be given to any of us we were disqualified. The rules included the usual accuracy and expression in the musical selection preformed but also our demeanor, stage decorum, sense of confidence and professionalism. When we walked onto the stage we needed to hold our bodies erect, arms straight though relaxed, heads held high and looking directly ahead as though we could see where we were going and walk directly to the spot at the front right hand corner of the concert grand piano to then slide into place.

The competition came all too soon for the Professor, but not for me. I knew I was ready. So did Grace. The day was a Saturday and Mama and Inger came to hear me. I couldn't see or talk with them until the end, when the scores were in. There were twenty-nine of us in the competition and all of those were performing either on the piano or the organ. Students came from schools all over the state. Excitement was high in the group from the School for the Blind. This was the first type of testing for me to be matched with others who could see.

Grace and I, both, had new voile dresses with satin ribbon someplace on the bodice or maybe tied at the waist. As it was getting harder to find Grace's waist with her girth expanding without limitation, an empire waistline was perfect for her. Obesity meant nothing to Grace for she was, as always, her jovial, quipping self, rarely, almost never serious.

I was always there for her, to say just the right thing for a wise-crack from her. Papa said we were like Mutt and Jeff, you know, in the funny papers, always a team although a very strange one. Without consciously trying, I just naturally handed her the lines to get a hilarious flash of syllables in return. And she did have a way with words.

Three of us girls from the school were entered in the state piano competition, so the Professor and Mrs. Trebing were able to drive us over in their car. As we got into their car inside the garage down at the bottom of the school lot, I heard Mrs. Trebing tell the Professor that a strange man was watching them across the street. He wasn't doing anything but just standing there, but she told him he had no purpose and no business in being there. The Professor told her not to pay any attention to him, that they had more important matters to think about.

As we drove to Little Rock's high school, he explained the rules of the contest. We understood and were challenged by having to be judged on a completely equal basis as the others. We all wanted to be were like everyone else. Certainly this was our chance to prove it. Earlier of that same week, we had been over to the school late in the day to test the stage. The Professor, with me in hand, had paced off the distance from the open curtain to the grand piano that was centered on the stage. It was eleven normal walking steps for me.

"Mrs. Trebing will position you girls at the curtain's edge in the direction to the right edge of the piano. Each of you will take the eleven steps at a casual and relaxed pace. On the eleventh step you should be able to touch the piano with your left hand. Do so with as little movement as possible."

"Oh, I don't need any help at all," I knew I could do it easily.

"You don't need any assistance but we must plan for the possible tension and stress of the moment. You could be thrown off, so please do exactly as we practice this."

He continued. "When you are able to feel the piano, either with your hand or with your leg, or foot, move sideways in between the piano and the bench. Think about what you're doing. You can do it without the batting of a hummingbird's wing."

"Even me?" inquired the obese Grace.

"Even you, my little owl," said the Professor.

"And I know you'll all move with the grace of a gazelle."

Grace quipped, "A grazing gazelle then goes gracefully galloping across the grain height green grass."

She was always saying those things, and as always, we all laughed. Mrs. Trebing cleared her throat to bring my mind back to the rehearsal.

"Now, let's try it. Ruth, you go first. And I then want you to sit down and play your piece. Let's make this a complete rehearsal. You'll need to get a sense of the pianoalities."

"What's THAT?" I frowned.

"Every piano has a personality. Their actions are different, some have stronger treble ranges, and others have a fuller bass range. You need to be aware of that in order to color your rendition correctly, as you would intend to do."

I walked to where Mrs. Trebing's voice was. I knew exactly where that was and stopped just before running into her. Mrs. Trebing softly called out. "Good. Check the direction of the curtain for a sense of the front of the stage."

My hands followed the wide curtain for just a few seconds to get my perspective. Then I went back to the side of the stage.

"Remember to stay out of sight of the audience, so back up a couple of feet from the outer edge of the curtain. You probably should add at least one step to your count forward to the center of the stage. Now, let's try it."

With my back straight and standing tall, I tried to walk as if I had been walking with a book on my head, level and still, counting to myself. One, two, three . . . At the count of twelve I stopped, gently lifting up my left arm. Sure enough, I was right at the piano. My hand touched the right side of the music rack as I was instructed. Edging sideways, the front of the keyboard brushed my thigh as the front of the bench pressed gently into the back of my leg. I took my time and stood for just a few seconds, and then moving in to where I judged to be the center of the bench. I then sat down.

My right hand moved across the black piano keys until I reached the two standing alone in the center of the keyboard. Just to their left would be middle "C," if I was in the middle of the keyboard. My left hand stretched out to follow the keyboard to its end. It could completely un-nerve a person to start out in the wrong place on the piano. Reaching that, my judgment told me I was indeed in the middle of the keyboard.

I began to play, the slow, deliberate beginning of the Chopin Nocturne. I leaned my body forward to give the support of power for my number. That was just like the Professor taught me to do. I relaxed and moved gently back and forth into the fast and light, middle section of the Nocturne. I didn't miss a note. It was almost like my hands were unattached from the rest of my body. I hit the keys with total accuracy and could lose myself in the expression of the work.

None of my classmates said a word, but sat in total concentration until I was finished. They all clapped. Professor Trebing spoke.

"Play it just that way at the competition. I promise you'll be a winner."

I knew it was good. I moved out of the bench area and turned to square off at a 90 degree angle. That's the way to get my bearings at the piano's edge. My exit into the wings was perfect.

On Saturday for the real thing, I was a little anxious but otherwise confidant. I was the first of the blind students to play, although the fourth of the competitors to perform. Mrs. Trebing gave me the signal and I moved forward across the stage. One of the mothers of another contestant suddenly realized that I was blind. She rushed across the stage to meet me and grabbed my arm to lead me to the piano. I pulled my arm away, but she had a firm grasp on it, saying, "Its all right, Honey, I'll help you."

There was nothing I could do. She had ruined my part in the competition and I was angry and so frustrated.

"No, no!" Mrs. Trebing said in quiet from her position just off stage.

"What's wrong?" the Professor asked.

"All our stage practice has been for nothing," Mrs. Trebing was so dejected.

"A woman took it upon herself to help her Ruth into place."

She could see the judges on the front row. They were speaking in a huddle, back and forth, and settled back into their seats as I began to play. The Professor later told me he was impressed by my maturity and understanding of the Chopin work. He was very pleased, but cautious about my rating as it was clear there would be equal evaluation, not only on performance but on stage decorum.

Sure enough, I was disqualified. The Professor explained that the woman acted on her own, through no invitation from either me or him. He argued. But the decision of the judges was final; therefore, I was not rated at all.

I was devastated. Why couldn't she have left me alone? We all thought the decision was unfair and the more I stewed about it the more determined I became to win first place next time. I turned that failure into work, hard work. I gave more time to both the piano and the pipe organ, for I was to play both in the student recital at Christmas and at the end of the school year. I'd be ready for the competition the next year and I was determined to win it.

CHAPTER FOURTEEN

Traveling Alone

For several years the trips to and from Little Rock for Ruth's weekend visits home, were always accompanied by me or another family member. If Peter was available he just hooked up his old horse, whom we fondly named Moose (due to his ears being unusually long for a horse,) to the buggy and the three of us made a nice Sunday outing as we rode over the Arkansas River bridge. Anna married her old boy friend and moved back to St. Louis, and the other two, Esther and Inger, each had their own friends and separate interests and were usually busy on Sundays. For the pick-up on Friday afternoon, Inger or I would ride the street car to the school to get Ruth. We'd return the same way. As time went by and she grew more independent, learning the system for getting around Little Rock by public transportation was important for her development and sense of confidence. The street car line ran from just a block away from our home, across the Main Street bridge to Fifth Street, a central hub for the cars running throughout the city. Only one change was required to reach the school from our apartment and that was made at the turn-around even though she was continuing in a straight line south on Main Street to the school. The car she was on from Arjenta simply circled around and returned across the river. There was no first street. The very first street was named Markham but all the others starting from Second were numbered and went to Eighteenth, where the School for the Blind was situated.

Grace Davenport stayed at the school for her week-ends. Her home was in Oklahoma. Her mother had died and her father, seemingly forever recovering from her mother's death, kept himself absorbed in his work in the state legislature. Grace had no brothers of sisters. She was able to have special holidays with her father and his family of many relatives, but that was mainly on Thanksgiving, Christmas and Easter. Otherwise, she remained at the school on weekends.

Inger's friends were always gracious and kind to Ruth but after she responded to their request to "play a number" for them they all went out on their merry way to wherever they were going. They never asked Ruth to go along. This was a great disappointment to her. At first I excused it as Ruth's being the little sister. Eventually I came to realize that many folk are not completely comfortable with anyone who's blind. It's like she might fracture like glass. Maybe they don't know if they should help her and if they ever tried, her independence would most certainly put them down in a rude-like manner. We, her family, certainly knew of the way Ruth waltzed around, up and down stairs, mounting and dismounting street cars and her generally smooth and graceful movement. Never-the-less Ruth was almost never included in her sister's dates. This widened the gap between her being like the others and having something wrong with her. Again, she always wanted to be like everyone else.

Grace's visits to our house relieved some of that tension for Ruth's being left out of her sisters' party plans and still provided some companionship for Ruth. None-the-less, since Ruth and Grace were together for most of the hours of each day during the week, Peter and I thought it unwise to have Grace with us every week-end.

The school was trying to prepare her for her adult life, not just of making a living and supporting herself, or to get married and have a family but to be able to move around independently, to shop and travel alone. We began training for solo street car riding on one of those weekends Grace was with us. Inger and I went with them through the passage across the river, sitting some distance away from them on the car. Then we remained until they boarded the correct street car to the school, listening to them giving the conductor instructions on seeing

them off at their school stop. The street names (or numbers) were
called out at each stop and they, just by listening, were counting all the
streets from the start to their point of debarkation. They had developed
a good sense of direction and of the amount of time to travel out to the
school. Both girls were well aware of where they were at all times. It
helped that the streets of both Little Rock and North Little Rock were
laid out on a grid and I can believe they had that map recorded in their
brains. Even so, we were not hasty in allowing them to travel alone
throughout the area.

Grace was my charge for this process. Inger took Ruth. By previous
agreement Inger and I were not to direct but to sit by and observe,
unless, of course, we were needed. This lesson in *finding the school*
proceeded without a hitch. I encouraged them to think on their own
rather than share information with each other. We teased them about
their advanced degrees in *direction finding* and *mental maps* and even
prepared little gifts for the graduation ceremony of this process. At
dinner that night, we drew placement cards with each girls name on it
followed by both DF and MM (for direction finding and mental maps.)
This tickled Ruth and Grace. And they were the first to tell Peter about
their accomplishment this first time and wanted to test us on other trips
later on. At 15 year of age, it was time for her father and me to know
when we could let go and let her go places by herself. This type of
independence was encouraged by both Peter and the school. In fact on
school hikes, sensory awareness and echo and sound identification were
discussed.

Eventually, we took that one step further by traveling alone from
downtown Little Rock and even later, put her on the street car close to
the house. The conductor on that car was used to the students at her
school so he saw to it that she successfully made the transfer to the
correct car at the terminal.

This form of transportation to and from home had already
become a pattern, for over a year, at the time when the small group
moved the Professor's car around inside the garage. Gradually, she
was able to make the entire trip alone. Being extremely intuitive
about the meaning of sounds being made around her, she knew our

neighborhood very well and could handle going back and forth to school confidently.

By four o'clock on Sunday afternoon, she would take her valise of fresh laundry and kiss her Papa and me goodbye, walk down the stairs to the street. She hung fairly close to the solid wall of the windowless brick building of the corner store, just under our flat. At the end of the wall she made a right turn and moved past the glass windows on each side of the store's entrance. The store was always closed on Sundays. That day of the week was usually fairly free of pedestrian traffic. Sometimes there were children playing out in their yards, or neighbors moving in or out of their homes or sitting idly on front porch swings as they chatted with family and friends. Two story homes lined that block from the store to the end of the block, except for the vacant lot at the corner of Main Street. Well-established locust trees were planted in about a two foot strip between the wooden sidewalks and the street's edge.

Ruth knew specifically where each of those locust trees was. She was also totally accurate in the position of each of the homes on the block. That was, perhaps, from her mental observations and the information she had wheedled out of her papa that the lots were all the same size, the houses on the lots were always directly in the middle, and the entrances to those homes were always in the center of the house. Many people thought this ability was so rare.

I don't remember that we ever had her touch these things, the trees and such, but Ruth just knew where things were. The trees on her side gave her a knowledge of the edges of both the sidewalk and the street. The trees continued in front of the vacant lot and it was, being a corner lot, extra wide.

She had paid attention to that because of walking past so many times with one of the members of our family. When she reached the corner, she waited for the sounds of the horses' hooves and the street cars to pass. There were very few automobiles on the streets by this time, easily identifiable by the put-put of their motors.

Ruth was very adept at this. Certainly, I would never have let her make this trip until I was absolutely certain of her ability to travel alone. Even though she did well with Grace, I needed to practice with her many times before she took the trip without us. Even then, for the first few tries at it, I followed a distance behind to watch. People frequently stopped her to chat but she never was distracted or thrown off her position by this. There were times when the children, understanding how she moved and having heard their parents talk about her, played games with her with placing themselves at the end of the row of trees, hoping she would *count* them as a tree. She laughed with them and it was all great fun.

One lovely sunny day in early April, Peter was called out into the country on an emergency. "Babies never make appointments," Doc explained. "I just juggle my plans, eat a few less suppers and bow to their demanding schedules."

"I'm sorry, Ruth. I was looking forward to a nice ride back to the school with you and your mother."

"That's alright, Papa. This is a good day to start to make the trip all by myself."

On the first reaction, I was cautious. But then, trying to put my over-protectiveness in place, I was able to rationalize that she was, indeed, ready. "Well, you have to start to be grown-up sometimes. I guess today is as good as the next."

Her Papa Doc (we added "doc" to his name as soon as he got his degree,) was preparing his bag for his pending delivery, when she kissed him goodbye. Then I handed her the packed valise of her clean clothes and off she went, full of self-confidence and enthusiasm.

A couple of men who probably were on the corner, hoping the grocery would be open, interrupted their conversation when she approached.

"Afternoon, Miz Ruth," one called out.

"Afternoon, Miz Ruth," echoes the second.

While she didn't know the men, she recognized them as having heard their voices around in the neighborhood. She knew they were black men from the sound of their voices. "Maybe they helped Mr. Halseys in his store. Papa has so many black patients. Maybe they're his patients," she thought. It didn't matter. They were always so kind and considerate of her and she was always very comfortable with them.

Ruth moved on down the sidewalk toward the end of the block. The Assaderians were on their front porch. The Mrs. was in the squeaky swing and he was rocking in a wooden chair. It made a soft wood-on-wood sound. They must have seen her coming.

"On the way back to school, Ruth?" Mrs. Assaderian called out. Without waiting for an answer, she continued with, "It's a lovely spring day, isn't it?"

"Hello, Ruth," Mr. Assaderian called out.

"Hello to you both. And to Mrs. Assaderian, yes it is a lovely day. Those young birds in your front tree sound like they're just babies, looking for their supper, maybe. Are they robins?"

Mr. Assaderian said, "Why, you're right. I hadn't noticed them."

"Yes, you're right, Ruth. They are robins." She paused as if she was searching for the activities up in the tree. "And, yes again, I think they're quite young."

"Yes, I do, too. Their voices are so soft, like they haven't had too much experience with their vocal cords. I'm trying for the 3:50 car into Little Rock. Excuse me for hurrying on." And she left them.

"How did she know those birds were up there?" Mr. Assaderian asked. "I didn't even know it and I've already been out here for over an hour." He continued. "You can't tell me she's blind."

Laughing, Mrs. Assaderian chided. "Come on, Harry. She listens to the sounds around her. How do think she gets around so well?"

"Well, she gets around better than I do."

"Of course she does," Mrs. Assaderian cracked. "She doesn't have arthritis like you do and she gets a lot of exercise, and she's young, and she pays attention like you don't. You're so used to ignoring me that you don't hear anything else, either," she whined.

He changed the subject and became very quiet as he thought about their blind neighbor. Maybe, it was that the wind moved unhindered through the vacant lot at the corner. Ruth knew she was passing it. She listened for the street sounds to tell her when she had reached its edge. There was a wagon just passing. There were several voices coming from it, probably a family of husband and wife and a teenage boy or two. There were four sets of hooves. Coming in the other direction was only one set of hooves.

"That would be a buggy, but since that's on the other side of the street-car tracks, I don't need to be concerned about it."

She listened for the sounds of the cars on the rails. They were in the far distance. After the second set of hooves passed directly in front of her and not hearing any other dangers close by, she walked briskly to the center of the street. She was sure she was in the center when she crossed the second set of tracks. Both sets vibrated, at different rates, giving her approximate distances of the street-cars from that point. The one she was to take, heading toward the river, was the strongest. It wasn't far away so she wouldn't have to wait long.

A lady was at her elbow as the street-car stopped almost directly in front of her. Gently, taking Ruth's arm, "Right up this way, Honey."

Ruth could smell alcohol on her breath. No liquor was sold on Sundays. The saloons were also closed. Ruth wondered about it. "It's stale. The alcohol is old. I think she had a lot to drink last night. She's probably got all sopped up and has just gotten out of bed, but no matter."

"Thank you for your kindness," Ruth moved her head to face the lady next to her. "I'll be quite able to make it on my own, now. Thank you again."

As Ruth climbed aboard the street-car and handed her coin to the conductor, he offered that the seat just behind him was vacant. "Sit right down here, Miss. You goin' clear across the river?"

"Yes, and would you please see me to the car going on Main Street south to my school? I'd be much obliged, if you would,"

The conductor announced the first stop south of the river. Ruth already was aware that the car had passed over the water because the sound was different than when it was traveling on solid ground. The space underneath the bridge created an echo like a ripe watermelon when "thumped" by my finger. Or like the noise the Doctor gets when he taps his fingers on my chest. Her stop was six blocks after the river so she expected it and began to prepare to rise with her valise in hand as soon as it was called.

It was then only twenty minutes after four. Lots of daylight remained. Many people were already on the street car when the new conductor led her down to the third seat back.

"I need to get off at the School for the Blind at Eighteen and Main streets. Please, let . . ."

"Sure will," he interrupted. "We'll take good care of you on this car, we will. Now, don't you worry your pretty little head, Missy.

He was gone.

Just as the *All aboard* was called out, Ruth felt somebody brush up against her in her seat. It was a large person who sat next to her. Probably a man, judging by the height, and a not-too-clean man, judging by his body odor. He breathed heavily, with kind of a snort when he exhaled.

"Probably, the car's full," she thought. "I hear children in the back, but I think they're not blind children, judging by the way they're moving about. They're not well behaved. I wonder if their parents are with them."

She was aware the man next to her was looking at her, because she could feel his breath when he turned to face her.

"That was quite a trick you'uns played on your teacher last fall, Lil lady."

Taken off guard, she answered, "What trick?"

"Oh, ya know. All you kids down at the garage, a turnin' his car around." His mouth odor was of decay and poor hygiene. I was uncomfortable with him.

"How do you know about that?

"Oh, I was a watchin' you all the time. I was a watchin' from across the street. I see you over there all the time."

"Oh." She said nothing else. She didn't want to encourage him in any way.

He went on. "Yeah, you're a right pretty little lady. You know that?"

She didn't answer.

He continued. "The Professa's a friend of mine. We's been friends for a long time. Yep."

"How do you know him?" Ruth was very doubtful.

"Oh, I work there at the school once in a while."

"Doing what?"

"Bringin' in the materials into the manual arts department. Yep, that's where I see him. He sure knows his business, he does."

Ruth knew he was lying. Why would Professor Trebing EVER be down in that department? The observatory was on the third floor. The manual arts department was in a separate building on the first floor and on the other side of the school.

She was uncomfortable with him, VERY uncomfortable. He was blocking her in. She couldn't just get up and leave to another part of the car. In the background of her hearing she was listening to the streets being called out as they approached the school. She knew they weren't far away.

"Now, don't you worry, Lil' lady. I'm goin' to take care of you today. I'll see that ya git back to tha school, right where ya belong. You just stay close to me, your new friend."

"No, thanks," Ruth defied him.

"Oh, no matter. When I sez he'll take care of ya, I means what I sez. Just leave it to me?"

"SCHOOL FOR THE BLIND" came the call from the front. And not a minute too early, either.

She got up from her seat. Her seat-mate didn't move and he was blocking her way.

"This is my stop," she said to him.

"Oh yeah. Well, ya come with me, Lil' lady."

"This is the stop for the blind school," repeated the conductor. Ruth could tell from the strength of his voice that the conductor had turned to face those behind him.

"Conductor," she called out. CONDUCTOR."

Standing and turning to the man at her side, "Please let me out." she ordered.

"This is my stop, conductor."

"I'm waitin for you, Miss," answered the conductor.

"I thank you," said Ruth.

Turning to face the obnoxious man at her side, "Sir, PLEASE LET ME OUT."

The conductor walked back to her. "Is there a problem here?"

The man next to her was already on his feet. "No problem. No problem a 'tall," he said calmly and quietly."

"Conductor, would you tell me if there are others getting off here who are obviously going to the school."

Apparently looking out on the street, since all those leaving at this point were already out, he said, "Why, yes, there are a couple of parents with some young children."

"No need, Lil lady, I'll take ya right to the door," said the smelly seat-mate.

Completely ignoring him but afraid of his persistence, she continued, facing the conductor's voice. "Oh, please. Please stop them and ask if I may walk with them into the school."

The conductor, now suspicious of her seat-mate, took Ruth by the arm and walked her to the front exit door of the car, calling over to the people already on the sidewalk.

"'Cuse me. You over there, 'cuse me. The young lady would like to walk with you to the school."

They waited and Ruth realized she knew them as soon as she heard the voices of their children. Oh, she was relieved. Thank God, they were there.

CHAPTER FIFTEEN

RUTH:
Excitement At The School

I didn't wait for the week end to tell Papa about the man on the street car. Telephones had gotten more popular, now. Of course, Papa had to have one for his practice and in cases of emergency at school, we were permitted to use the phone in the registration office. Papa told me he would call the Superintendent, Mr. Traeger. He made the report himself. Afterwards, Mr. Traeger wanted to hear my story of the incident. He called me to his office out of my Public Speaking class and when I got there, Miss Hanker, his secretary, was just walking out the door of the outer office. "Someone is with him at this time and I need to run an errand, but I'll be right back. Take a seat and wait for him."

I sat right down in the chair next to the closed door of his office. But I think it wasn't closed so well because when Miss Hanker left the room and closed the outside door, the metal piece that locks the door into closed position made a clicking sound. Evidently this loosened the door latch because I could then hear the voices inside his office more clearly. At least two boys were in with Mr. Traeger and he wasn't talking to them about the school or their studies, what they'd done, or anything like that. It was a curious conversation. The more I listened, the more I realized that I wasn't supposed to hear any of it.

"Boys, I need it bad, a shot in the arm REAL bad. I just haven't been able to get away from here. Do you think you could help me out, get down to Lee's Pharmacy for some dope?" (Why would the Superintendent ask those boys for a 'shot'? Why not Papa or another doctor in town? And I didn't understand 'dope'. He asked the boys for dope.)

"Yessir, Mr. Traeger."

"You're sure? You boys can get it for me, huh?" That was the Superintendent talking.

"We're sure. But what's in it for us? And anyway Mr. Lee wants the money for it first. We don't have it." I recognized that voice, too. It belonged to Jimmy James. He was not one of my favorite people. I got a creepy feeling about him, like a worm crawling up my finger, like I wanted to stay away from him.

"What's he getting for morphine?" the questions continued. (OH, that I understood.)

"I don't know. Do you want coke or morphine? Neither one's ever on Ma's shopping list." Jimmy snickered.

"Yeah, cocaine'll be a buck fifty for what you usually get." That was Ivan Oddsky, another student. I'd know his voice anywhere. I'd had algebra with him last year and he flunked. He was a real tough kid, lived in the hollow down by the river where the squatters are. He was an older student, probably grown by now. If I could remember how long ago it was that his voice changed. Yes, it was at least 5 years ago. I didn't like him. I didn't know anyone who did.

"I really need something bad," Mr. Traeger voice sounded shaky. "If you can't get coke, get me what you can. You boys go right on down now. I'll take care of your class."

My gosh, they are talking about drugs. Mr. Traeger was buying drugs. Why? He's using drugs himself and getting those boys to buy them for him. It wasn't illegal to use morphine or cocaine but it was a well known fact that 'nice people' didn't use drugs. I thought the only people who used drugs when they weren't sick were gangsters and hooligans. Those were the kind of people who used drugs? On second thought, I remember that Sherlock Holmes took morphine, but not a teacher. Certainly not the superintendent of my school. I heard him. What I heard was clear. There's no mistaking about what I heard. Well really, I know he wanted to buy drugs. But he'd only buy them to use, himself. 'Said he needed it "real bad." Or maybe, he was selling them, too. Oh, my goodness, was he selling drugs?

What would happen to me if they knew I'd heard them? I had to get out. Nobody could know that I heard what they were negotiating. So I got up and quickly and quietly walked over to the door, opening it very carefully. I shut it behind me in total silence. I walked down to the end of the hall and stood in the warmth I knew as sunlight, pouring through the tall pane of glass. I needed to think. Did our superintendent use drugs or was he dealing drugs

"Through already?" It was Miss Hanker. I jerked around. I had not heard anyone approaching. "I, I, I came out here to wait. I don't feel so good and I . . ."

"You don't look so good. Your face is all flushed. You'd better have Miss Minnie look you over," she said. "Why don't you go on over to the infirmary and come back here when you feel better."

"Yeah. I'll go to the infirmary and come back here later," I said.

Of course, there was nothing wrong with me so I only went into the infirmary and told Miss Minnie that I wasn't feeling too well, and that it was my time of the month, so she'd understand and let me go right away. "But I feel better now," I told her. She insisted that I lie down for a few minutes. That was really fine with me because I needed the time and quiet place to think.

I was originally called into the Superintendent's office. He wanted to see me and eventually, I'd have to go in and talk with him. I knew he wanted to ask me about the man on the street car. "Get it over with," my inside voice said. I tried to relax as I curled up on the infirmary cot.

"Take this, Miss Minnie was standing over me with a pill and a small cup of water. I took it and waited for about 30 minutes, until I was a bit more relaxed and then left.

Later, in Mr. Traeger's office, I answered his questions about the man on the street car. He seemed unusually agitated and harried.

"Sorry, you don't feel so well today," he said. His questions were brief, surprisingly brief. In fact, he only asked me when it happened and if I recognized the man. I said, "no" and he let me go.

Whom should I tell about the conversation I'd overheard between the superintendent and the two boys? Should I say anything to anyone? Grace is my best friend and I've got to tell someone. I told Grace. Together, we decided not to tell anyone else. That is, for the time being.

Our secret-telling seriousness was suddenly overshadowed by several of the girls snickering in a huddle just outside in the hall. They were blocking our path and I, at least, needed to have a change of thought.

"Hey, what's going on out here," Grace asked. It seems, according to them, that some of the students had "borrowed" the school wagon which was left standing on the road down at the farm. That was the acreage on the lower end of the school property which included an orchard of fruit trees and several acres of crops planted with vegetables for our table. I never liked it down there because all our compost was taken down there to season so it really smelled foul.

It seems the wagon was just sitting in the road with the two horses in place on the front while the workmen were over in the field. One of the boys said. "Anyone want to go for a spin?" Six or seven of our boys scrambled into the wagon almost like their feet were on fire. One of the farm boys picked up the reigns and they began to move. He snapped the leather across the backs of the two horses. The wagon rolled on and picked up speed as the boys whooped and hollered like a bunch of wild Indians. Then they started down the hill with the curve right in the middle of it, but they were going too fast. The wagon shifted to two wheels and then tipped and rolled over. The boys were scattered about like a dropped package of dried beans, in the ditch and up the bank on the side, with the wagon landing on top of Angelo Petrilli. He was pinned underneath the wagon. His leg was broken. One of the horses couldn't stand on his leg. If it was broken he'd probably have to be shot.

Everybody on that wagon was hurt, either cut, broken or bruised. One of the boys split his head open when he was thrown out against a tree trunk. Someone fetched Miss Minnie and she organized the emergency aid with temporary bandages and had Angelo carried into the infirmary.

His broken leg became a status symbol. At first, all the boys were pretty scared because they took the wagon without permission and there were injuries. They knew they'd be punished, but by the time they were hauled into the superintendent's office for their penalties, it was known the horse would not have to be destroyed and Angelo's leg would eventually be all right. Of course, they were put on detention but by that time their little escapade was the talk of the school and it appeared their joy ride became worth the punishment. The distraction in it was worth a lot to Grace and me at that time.

Papa was sick with a really bad case of the flu so I didn't tell my parents what I had heard in Mr. Traeger's outer office. Mama was very tired taking care of Papa so I decided to wait until next week to tell them. I needed to tell them as soon as possible because I knew good people didn't use those kind of drugs. Certainly nice people would never involve the students in drugs. I wasn't sure what Mama and Papa would think or do if I told them, so I put it off for the time being.

That next Sunday, I returned to the school after a good afternoon buggy ride. An early frost had taken the fall's Indian summer two steps ahead, so it was a little chilly. Alice missed supper that night. By bedtime she still hadn't come in. I know it was past midnight when the Black Widow came in for a bed check. Alice had never missed bed check before, at least not while I was at the school. I went right back to sleep figuring she just stayed home and her parents were slow to advise the school. By morning, the word was around that Alice was missing.

Someone said that her brother reported that he'd ridden out with her on the street car about 5:30 Sunday evening. But as they approached the school stop, he spotted the return trolley car coming toward them so he got out at the corner just before the school. Alice had insisted that she could walk the last block alone and so she got out at the same time. Alice began walking on the sidewalk toward the school while her brother bolted for the trolley to go back home She didn't come to school on Monday morning, either. All the houses close by had been checked for any information the police could get on Alice. Nobody claimed to have seen her. By noon, the police were organizing a posse to look for Alice. They started at the corner where her brother said he had left her.

Everyone at the school were really scared by now. It was morose, like a mausoleum or funeral parlor. The rainstorm that morning reflected all of our fear and sadness. That is, the mood inside was morbid but outside, we could hear the voices of several men walking the grounds. I could hear their voices up close to the school and I could hear men's voices in the distance, too. There were many of them, all searching for Alice or some trace of her. We were all afraid, not just for Alice but for the rest of us. Where could she be? Where could she have gone and if she was lost, why hadn't she asked some one for directions? Why had nobody found her? It was hard to keep our minds on our studies but the instructors demanded that we continue.

Papa read about Alice's disappearance in the Wednesday morning Times and came directly to the school. He wanted to know first hand just how safe I was so he talked with Mr. Traeger and after that the police chief.

The paper said the police had picked up several clues on the school grounds. At the time we weren't aware of what those clues were but Papa later found out that they found an old sweater, two men's handkerchiefs (one of them a dirty white and the other a red bandanna), several hair pins, a hat pin with a mother of pearl droplet on the end, a cameo (usually worn with a black ribbon at the high neck of a lady's blouse) and the heel of a man's work boot. And the Chief was particularly pleased to have found a woman's black stocking like those all the girl students wore. He was sure it belonged to the missing girl. Papa called me out of class to tell me of his concern so I told him about the experience I'd had the previous Sunday on the street car. He knew Mr. Traeger certainly would have reported it and the police were acting on that information, but he went back to the superintendent's office to see about that. Traeger had done nothing about my report but said he'll talk to the police immediately. Papa said he was disappointed that Mr. Traeger was so passive about the incident on the street-car.

Alice still didn't show up by evening on Wednesday and Papa wouldn't let me stay in school. He called Senator Davenport in Oklahoma City and got his permission to have Grace remain with us, at least for the time being.

The tension of her disappearance increased throughout the week as Alice failed to show up either at the school or at home. The speculation on the kind of person who would kidnap a blind girl got pretty wild and fear gripped the school and the city. Both Grace and I spent time practicing on the piano at home but neither of us had our minds on our music. I was afraid for Alice. Grace said she was a bright girl and would not have gotten lost by getting off the car that close to the school. We both knew that she had no boy friends at the school and everyone liked her. What happened to her?

Papa called to see if Grace and I would come down to his office and make pills for him. We accepted his offer immediately, grateful for the distraction. I knew that was precisely why he asked. He just wanted to keep us busy because I had made pills for him just a little over a week ago. Mama was confident we could make the trip alone from the new home we were in to his old office but she said she "wouldn't allow it this time, not with a mad man running loose in the city."

I was used to making Papa's pills for him and was happy to show Grace how to make them. It was an easy job. Papa had pill presses and would give us the right sized press and the jar of the powdered medicine. "Just dip the tiny scoop into the powder and dump it on the press table. Then all you do is slap down the iron lid hard." When I opened the press, I showed Grace the finished pill, firm and compact. Then we'd count them into groups of 15 or 20, depending on the number Papa asked for, and put them into small envelopes to seal. Mama had pre labeled the packets for me to use when Papa needed them. I don't think Papa really needed them now but he just wanted to give us something to do. Papa took us back to our house with him at the end of the day.

The next day, we again went to Papa's office in the afternoon and cut and packaged his bandages for him. This was another of Papa's keep-busy projects. I'd made those three weeks ago and I knew he didn't need them this soon.

But by Saturday morning, the paper said the police were at a dead end. They had not found Alice and they were discouraged about the clues found on the grounds. Nobody knew anything about the sweater but it was so badly faded that it was felt it had been there a long time.

The woman's stocking the Chief was so happy to find was too small to have belonged to Alice, so that "clue" was eliminated. About the cameo, Alice's mother said her daughter wore nothing at her neck with her black school uniform. "The school doesn't allow it, you know. The girls must all be dressed alike."

At supper that night Papa said, "what did you tell the police, Ruth?"

"Nothing, Papa. I didn't talk with the police. You told me you'd talk to the superintendent. I guess you did because Mr. Traeger had me come in to his office and asked me some questions."

"And the police didn't talk to you about it?" he asked. When I again answered in the negative, he said as if under his breath, "hum, strange." He was probably deep in thought for he was silent for a full minute before he said. "The man who sat next to you on the trolley may have no relationship to Alice's situation. But, it's worth looking into. I'm going to call Chief Amos, myself."

It was less than an hour later that the chief and another policeman knocked at our door. Papa stayed in our parlor with me while I told the two men about the smelly man on the street car.

"Well, I'm glad you've told us about him. He may have nothing to do with Alice. And perhaps he does. We'll find that conductor and get a description of him. 'Any chance someone told you what this guy looked like?" he inquired.

"Nobody told me anything about him. Of course, I didn't ask, but I can describe him if you wish. He was a large man, probably over six feet tall. He wore overalls, and was dirty and unkempt."

"Oh, I'm sorry, Ma'am. I didn't realize you could see." Papa said the policeman twisted his head, squinted his eyes and looked harder at me and then stood back staring at my face.

"I'm blind, sir. That doesn't mean I can't see." I flashed back at him.

The chief's voice was controlled. "Oh, now, wait a minute, Ma'am. You don't make sense. You can't be blind and also see," he said forcefully. He slowly shook his head back and forth. "Now which is it?"

Papa interrupted the questioning. "You don't know much about our blind children, do you, Amos? They rely on their other senses when their eyes don't work. They believe they see and they do but in a different way than you and I are used to. Listen to what she has to say. You'll probably find her impressions very accurate."

Still disbelieving, he cautiously began his questioning again. "You say he was a big man. How do you know that?"

"Because he sat down right next to me. There is only room for two people on those wooden benches. You can see I'm rather thin and when he sat down he pushed up against me like there wasn't enough room for him.

He invited me to continue.

"He took up all the room and his shoulders extended several inches above mine. I'm five feet, four inches tall. I'd say he's about six feet tall."

"There's no way you can tell how tall he is just by him sitting next to you." This time it was the other officer who spoke.

"Sure, I can. When he spoke, his mouth was a lot higher than my ear. Remember, Officer, he was right next to me."

"But, now you can't know he was wearing overalls, Ma'am."

I snapped. "Officer, when you're interested in my information, you can contact me. At this point you don't believe anything I tell you. I see no point in continuing."

He seemed to be taken off guard by my forcefulness and sass. "Sorry, Ma'am, or Miss. I meant no disrespect. I'm a policeman, used to people who are norm . . ." He stopped.

"Normal people?" I said. "Is that what you were going to say?"

"I didn't mean that. Ah-a, can we start again.? You were saying about the overalls."

I said, "Oh yes, how did I know he was wearing overalls?"

"Because I touched the fabric when I leaned over to check on my loosened shoe. Certainly don't you know that overalls are worn for work? It's heavier and more coarsely woven than the twills that most trousers are made from, or thicker than the lighter weight material in my uniform, for instance."

He hesitated and then continued. "So far you're doin' fine, Little Lady. But dirt? You said he was dirty." I knew he put his head down and wagged it back and forth by the alternating strength of his voice. I still don't think he really believed me.

"Well, I can't say for sure that he was dirty. But the chances are his clothes were dirty." I forged ahead. "He hadn't taken a bath in many days. That I'm sure. The smell I picked up, was one of sweat on sweat, stale and stinky. And no fresh underwear, either." I wrinkled up my nose and made a frown.

Amused by that expression of disgust, he said, "Anything else?"

"Yes. He is either sick or has a strange habit."

"Like what?" The officer was on his toes.

"When he exhales, he makes a snorting sound. Maybe he needs his adenoids removed.

The officer began to laugh. "Oh, so now you're a doctor, too? You were doing okay there for a while, but now he has an adenoid problem."

I could hear Papa chuckling. He knew I learned something from his house calls that I went out on. Stiffening my back and trying to be patient, I explained.

"I make calls with my papa. He doctors at his office and out at people's homes. We talk. He tells me what he knows about, not just his patients, but the others around the sick people he's called out to tend. And I hear things differently from him so we talk about it. We kind of help each other."

"Well, I sure do thank you for your information, Miss Christensen. You've been a great help and you've also helped me."

They stood up and headed for the door.

"Oh, one more thing, Officer. I almost forgot. He chews tobacco."

He wheeled. "Now, you want to tell me how you could ever know he chews tobacco?"

"I could smell it, of course," I answered.

"Now, maybe he had been weeding in a field of tobacco. Or even he just walked through a field of tobacco."

"Officer." I stood up. I was going to make this man a believer yet. "Don't you know the smell of a fresh field crop is different than the deposit of the dried leaves mashed up in a mouthful of saliva?" I began to think he wasn't too bright. He just grunted and headed out the door.

Papa followed him out the door and down the stairs to the street.

At the street door, he said to them. "Chief Amos, tell me. Did you get a call about this man early last week?'

"Call? From who?" he asked.

"From the superintendent, you know, at the school, Mr. Traeger?".

"No, can't say that I did. Oh, hell, I'd of remembered it if I had, Doc. No I didn't hear from Traeger last week. Why do you ask?"

"Just wondering," Papa said.

"Anything else, Doc?"

"No, I'll call you if I think of anything else." He closed the door and came back upstairs.

When Papa came back into the kitchen, he could see that Mama and Grace were already in there with me. They'd heard everything I said from the other room. I said, "Papa, do you think the man on the street car might have any thing to with Alice?"

"I have no idea." He paused pensively, but the point is his behavior was very strange and suspicious in view of Alice's disappearance so soon afterward."

CHAPTER SIXTEEN

Alice Found

The authorities moved into high gear now with this new lead, the only strong lead they have at this point. They had to find the man who had sat next to Ruth on the trolley. Chief Amos took one man, Scotty, to go immediately to the office of the municipal transportation. He soon found out the name of the car conductor working on that car at the time of the incident with Ruth and was told it'd soon be time for his shift to end and he'd be reporting into the central office within 15 minutes. That was the small tower building just a few yards away, across several tract lines that lead out to the outlining area to service the growing city. They didn't wait long before the conductor they were looking for came in.

"Yeah, I know the man. He hangs around the school a lot, not right on the school grounds, mind you, but I see him just standing against a tree across the street, just watching the students from his position on the other side of the street. Now, he's not there at the beginning of my run. That's when the school is in session. It must be after hours when the kids are outside that he wants to be there."

"Do you know his name?" the Chief asked.

"No, and I don't think he works, or has a job or anything like that. He rides my car pretty often. I usually pick him up at the central station, . . . hum-m-m, maybe about three o'clock in the afternoon and he gets off at the school. He's slow moving. You know, has no energy, no pep. Sometimes, he doesn't ride with me and I see him walking back to town, like maybe he doesn't have the price of a fare. I believe I saw him riding an old nag once or twice, too. But he's always over on that side of town, always close to the school."

"We'll check with some of the other car-men. I'd much appreciate your help. Thank ya! Let me know if you think of anything else."

Two policemen remained in the municipal car-line office to get the names and addresses of all the other conductors. They'd all be talked to. By the time they left it was almost 2 a.m. On the trip back to the station the Chief let his thoughts flow out into words. "We've got a description of that guy but where do we look NOW, Charlie?" Without waiting for an answer, "Tell you what. You go on home now and get a little rest. I want to get out a poster with that guy's description. Maybe one of our people will know who he is. Meet me at the Blind School at eight in the morning." He was already setting the brake on his car at the station house as Scotty opened the door. He was stepping off the running board when Chief Amos called out to him. "Better phone Traeger before you go out and tell him you want to see him in his office at 8 o'clock in the morning. I want to spend some time there, looking for what I'm not sure yet but I need some direction and I think I'll start there."

At the school the next morning Traeger was in a most depressed state. The Chief watched him with curiosity as he fumbled and pulled out a list of students at the Chief's request. Traeger never seemed to face the policemen, but the one time that he did for just a second, Amos noticed his eyes seemed to show no pupil. They were all iris.

Almost as soon as he set it down in front of Chief Amos, he grabbed it, "'sa wrong one. Sorry. Here's the right list. Sorry! Sorry!"

Chief Amos was looking for any student whose home address might be close to Alice's. He asked which students were at the school over this last week-end, which ones might have been returning about the time Alice got off the trolley. One by one he went over who they were, where they came from, what their grades were like, how many friends they had in school, what were the teachers remarks about the student, general opinions about them, anything that might paint a picture of the student and his character. Was he or she a friend of Alice's? Were they enemies?

It was a pains-taking process, a long tiring process. Scotty took the list of teachers, then the employees, anyone making a delivery at that time, former students. Much of this had already been done by his men but everyone needed to be checked again. There was nothing that stood out.

They broke for the noon meal about 12:30 and walked down to the teachers' dining room. With the beginning of Sunday's dinner in his mouth, Chief Amos thought about the change in Mr. Traegor, for by this time he even quieter, more depressed. "What's going on with him?" he asked to himself. "Was he uncomfortable about answering our questions? If so, why? Look at him. He's eating, but not much. His appetite's not too good. And his color. Um-m, curious! And he avoids looking straight at me."

When lunch was over, the two policemen gave their "thanks" for the meal and excused themselves. They returned to town.

The Chief had drawn out a map of the School for the Blind to plot out the position of all the buildings, marking the usage of each structure where each clue was found and all the positions of each structure on the adjacent properties, if there were any buildings on them or was it only vacant land. The school was really out a distance from town, or at least it seemed to be so since the growth around it was slow. The street-car line extended beyond the school and I know there are people living further out. Of the out-buildings away from the center core of the school were, according to one of his men:

1. On the south side up close to the road was the house for the superintendent, set back a ways from the street, his garage behind it.

2. On the north side of the school right next to the main buildings was the laundry, the wood-house, maintenance shop and the butcher house. And closer to the street were three garages for staff cars, although only two were used.

3. In the rear was a dormitory used for overflow housing
    for teachers since the school had needed to employ
    more teachers.

A road turning off Main Street lead to the superintendent's house on the south side while on the north side, the road went the distance of the acreage of the school but was the service road for the equipment and material being delivered to the school from town. The same road was used to bring up farm products to the school's kitchen or storage coolers in the rear of the main building.

The superintendent's home housed his wife and had at one time been the home for his two boys, both of whom had been married and moved away. Mrs. Traeger was a very serious lady of rather pious beliefs, a strong Southern Baptist in good standing, who attended her church every Sunday mornings, evening worship the same day and "Prayer Service" on every Wednesday evening. At one time, her husband had also attended these services with her but now that the boys had left home, there was no longer any need to "set the example" and he preferred to enjoy the peace and silence of his home while the family "talker" was absent.

On the other side of the school, two of the three garages usually had vehicles of some kind inside, a tin lizzy or even a buggy. At least this was so when their owners had returned to the school after summer vacation. Since the majority of the students went home for the weekends, most of the staff could enjoy a day away from the school on those days also, as only a skeleton staff was needed for the remaining students. The road leading down to the farm was heavily used during the week and even on Saturdays, but not on Sunday.

The Chief asked for each man who had found a possible clue to mark its location on the map with a red circle. The cameo and two hairpins were found within three feet of each other and almost at a ninety degree angle from the farm road and about forty feet back off Center Street. The boot-heel had been found at the side of the farm road directly between the it the location of the cameo.

That was significant, the Chief thought, but the cameo does not belong to the missing girl. Yet, it was almost new. Alice's mother said Alice's cameo was new. The rain of Monday was probably its first exposure to water because of the condition of the pin.

"Was Alice on the wild wagon ride? I don't think so because all those kids were hurt someway and I don't remember her name on the injured list. But it must be checked and right now, that's the only thing we've got," the Chief pondered. Her trail ends here at the school. It's here that we must find where it picks up. After a minute's silence, he snapped to attention and began barking orders. "Clem, go on out to Alice's home and ask her mother to show you her cameo. Bring it in."

Turning to his other side, "Charlie and Elmer go back to the school and talk to every student, individually. Ask them for all Alice's contacts, what they've overheard, comments from Alice about who her friends are, her special friends and then spend some time with those friends. Somebody has to know something. Find it."

"Scotty, come with me. I want to see the lay-out where the heel was found." He bolted for the door, and just as he reached it turned back to Charlie. "'Better get a list of former students, too. Look at staff, particularly the ones that live at the school most of the time. Find out what you can on their history. I've already checked our reports. The names aren't familiar to me and there's nothing in our files before I came to the job."

A very careful survey was made of the area where the cameo had been found and the shoe heel was found not very far away. The Chief and Scotty paced it off, retraced the peripheral area from the trees to the road, pulled out some of the broken stems of weeds in the cameo area, examining closely. Then out to the road, both got to hands and knees so as not to miss a thing, any small item of importance. "Something happened here, Scotty. I can smell it. I know it."

Seeing the police car coming toward them, both men stood up and waited. It was Clem, racing up and braking quickly. "Alice's mother can't find her cameo. I think the one we found here belongs to her."

"Yelp. I think you're right. And I think someone carried her maybe limp or lifeless body, away right at this spot here," he said looking down.

It was a little after three o'clock in the afternoon when they finished and walked back to the police car left in front of the school's entrance. The Chief was already seated when Scotty walked around to the driver's side. As he got in, with excitement rising in his voice, "Take a look, Chief, over there across the street. It's the man we're looking for. It's HIM."

The Chief crossed the street quickly as the subject was glancing away from him, down the direction toward town. One hand was on his opened holster at his waist. Scotty wheeled a "U" turn, pulling right in front of the man just as the Chief said, "Fellow, you're going down to the station house with us. We need to talk."

On the way downtown, the Chief turned over to Scottie. "That description, you know the one from the blind girl, it's exact even down to the smell." They both began to laugh.

"Well, I'll swan," Scotty shook his head in disbelief.

The school was in turmoil when Alice was first declared to be "missing." As the days passed without her being found, fear seeped into a deeper level. It was fear for each of us, not just for Alice's fate (whatever that was) but for any and all of us. My fear turned to anger, anger at the man on the street car. I feared the unknown, at what others might be able to see out there but neither Alice or I could see. The villainous, dirty man who sat next to me on the street car, I came to despise. I hated with an intensity I'd not known before without even knowing he had anything to do with Alice's disappearance. He was the lowest of lows to take advantage of a blind girl. Grace and I remained at home with my parents.

Papa said I mustn't be too quick to convict the man on the street-car. "Just because he was a little problem to you doesn't indicate he had anything to do with Alice. He may not have ever heard of Alice. Wait until all the facts are known."

Grace and I had talked about what we knew about Mr. Traeger and decided we really needed to tell my parents about the conversation I had overheard from Traeger's office. This was a good time to tell him. Afterward, Papa said we should have told him right away after I heard it. He called Chief Amos and again he came to the house. After telling him everything I heard, he said, "Well, that behavior is a matter for the legislature. I don't think Mr. Traeger has anything to do with Alice and you realize that I've arrested that Luther man from the street-car?

That's the first time I'd heard his name. "What's his last n . . .". A hard knock at the front door jarred us all with alarm. It was an officer. We could all hear him for he just blurted out, "We found her. We have that blind girl, Chief. She's as dead as she'll ever be."

My mouth dropped open. I heard Grace gasp. Mama was already right in front of us, putting one arm around me, the other around Grace on the other side. She pushed our faces up against her as she stood in between us. Both us girls were numb, terrified, grief stricken, and angry.

Within an hour of the police finding Alice's body, the Arkansas Democrat had a "Special" out on the streets. Mama read us all the details that were in print. She was in a ditch just off the road, with no marks on her. Oh, there were some bruises, minor red blotches but no knife or bullet wounds. The suspicions were that she was strangled. No explanations or suggestions of how she got from the school to the ditch.

We were terribly upset; upset that our friend was dead, upset that her death was violent and we were afraid, too. Grace and I stayed awake long after we had gone to bed that night thinking and talking about what might have happened to her, and if she died in great pain and fear. No one else in the house slept much that night but at breakfast Papa seemed at ease when talked about it. He said he was confident the police would find whoever the murderer was. I think he was just trying to calm us.

Papa and Mama did take us out for a picnic the next afternoon. The October sun was still warm but we could smell rain in the air and other changes of autumn. The leaves were turning, Mama said, but few had fallen to the ground where we had our picnic. I told Mama I heard a goose in the air. "Papa said no, I didn't because it was too early."

With the whole school traumatized by her death and with the gossip about the superintendent, it became clear to the Professor and Mrs. Trebing that something needed to be done for the students. The

Trebings took a day off from the school and Mrs. Trebing drove their car down to Hot Springs to take the student's condolences to Alice's family. At the same time, it became evident to them that a funeral held at the school might be beneficial to the students left there, so they presented this suggestion to Alice's family. At first they declined. After an hour or so of hearing about and understanding their daughter's popularity and the love the students had for her, they changed their minds and consented.

The Professor already knew her favorite songs, her love of the different music they had worked on together. The funeral or memorial service at the school would involve as many of Alice's friends as possible. Ruth would play the Requiem on the organ and on the piano Grace played Mozart's Gloria from the Twelfth mass. The choir sang Nearer My God to Thee. It was all beautiful. Everyone came. And everyone gave their best performance for their fallen friend.

The family wanted an open casket, for this was the only service for their daughter. They wanted to be able to see her in peaceful sleep. We wanted to see her, too. As this became clear to the Trebings, Mrs. Trebing prepared us for that event. "Her body will be cold; cold and hard when the life has gone and rigor mortis has set in. Those of you who wish can look for yourselves but be prepared for this condition. With her family so close, it would be improper to recoil when you touch her. You think about it but understand what you will see." Many entered the line to file by the casket, reach in and touch her. Others avoided it. But the opportunity to see her in death was not denied us.

Both Grace and I wanted to see the casket and Alice. We took as much time as we needed to and nobody rushed us. Inside the wooden box, Alice was stretched out on a smooth satin sheet on a puffy mattress. She was in a dress that must have been prettier than our uniforms because the material was a lighter weight and she had a band of lace at her wrist and neck. I touched her hand. It was not like a hand. The skin was tight and she was so cold. I wanted to see her face too but even though Mrs. Trebing warned us, I couldn't touch her again. I sat down after that.

I felt I had given her my best gift, the gift of my music. I think the others did also. My anger was still there but this began the healing process. I was angry at Mr. Traegor. Papa said special meeting of the legislative committee was being called to discuss his future at the school. (The trustees of the school were the State's legislative body.)

Papa made sure he was able to come to the school to pick me up on that next Friday afternoon. He was always so attuned to my feelings. I was very quiet for most of the ride home. When he did talk, I became angry at him and spoke rudely to him. Usually, that would not be tolerated in our family. This time he let it go. He understood. For once, I didn't have to do the dishes after supper. Inger did. But Papa said he wanted to talk with me in his office.

Mama had a wonderful supper that night, all my favorite things. I loved chocolate layer cake with thick chocolate frosting and she served that for dessert. I helped scrape the leavings from the dishes and stack them for washing when Papa called me in.

Basically, he only wanted me to talk. Talk about Alice, of how I would remember her, of the fun times we had. I began to laugh when I talked about our parade through the chapel on that early morning escapade. "Alice had said the raiding party in the chapel was more fun than putting watermelon slices down the backs of other students. And she lavished in the event when we all relived it for a group of curious students."

I talked about the man on the street car and Papa reminded me that I had taken care of myself at that time, just like he always told me too. "Pay attention to your feelings. Depend on them," he would say. "And you did. See how well you do on your own?"

That was a nice compliment. I appreciated it but I became angry again when we began to talk about the murderer of my friend. I was also angry at Mr. Traeger and said so, too. Papa said he thought Mr. Traeger was unsuitable for the job at the school and would soon be relieved of his duties.

"At this time," he said. Papa spoke so calmly as his voice was soft and slow. "Mr. Traeger will be punishing himself for many a year. The man has a whole set of problems I wouldn't wish on my worst enemy. Let him go and forget him."

Papa's gentleness did little to soothe me as I burst out, "I don't want to be blind. I didn't want Alice to be blind. It's not fair! Why did Alice have to be blind, Papa? Why do I have to be blind?"

He moved from his swivel chair over to the bench next to me and put his arm around my shoulders. He alternately wiped my face with his handkerchief and replaced the straggling hairs back on top of my head. He was very tender. He just sat close with his arm around me. After a while he spoke.

"Life is not always fair, Ruth. Many things happen to many people that aren't fair. But that's just the way life is and there's nothing we can do about it. There are some things we simply must accept and go on to make the best of it."

He relaxed his arm on my shoulder but he picked up my hand to hold as he straightened up his body.

"When you were first born, and your sight destroyed, we thought it was so unfair, like fate had played a bad trick on you. And on us. I know that's not true. All things happen for a purpose, a purpose we don't know at the time."

I calmed down some and began to relax. He continued. "You're our pearl, Ruthie, your mother's and mine." He spoke with great tenderness. I knew this was what he truly believed. "You're as precious as a pearl, as valuable as a pearl, the finest pearl."

I could feel his breath on my cheek as he turned to face me. He asked, "Do you know how pearls are made?"

"They come from the sea," I replied.

"Yes," he said. "They do come from the sea. They grow inside a clam. Pearls are very precious. They're gems of great beauty. In their natural state they have an iridescent luster. That means, they show themselves in many colors based on the different lights around them at the time. Nobody needs to polish them in order to see or enhance their beauty. They're always beautiful and certainly are very precious."

"Pearls are round without sharp edges so there's no need to have facets cut into their sides like a diamond or ruby. They come in many different shapes. Most of the time they are smoky white or almost white. But I understand they can be pink or a dark gray, too."

I tried to imagine what a pearl would look like. I do think Papa could read mymind because he said. "Do you remember before you got sick and you could see a little light? And sometimes in that light there were colors?"

He continued. "For hundreds of years kings and the great sheiks of Arabia have bought pearls for their crowns or in rings, or matched in colors and sizes to be strung on a string around the necks of their queens. I'm just getting to the most interesting part of the pearl story. Pearls only exist because of an accident." Again he turned toward me, "Did you know that, Ruth?"

"I don't understand," I squeaked out.

"Well, there are actually two ways the accident could happen that produces a pearl. One is from a grain of sand and the other is a little parasite. Either way, the sand or parasite works its way in through the tightly closed shells. The clam can't get rid of it, the intruder. It can't cough it up so the clam begins to encircle that intruder with a hard coating, similar to the inside of its shell. So that newcomer inside the shell continues to grow as the clam adds more and more coats of its own skin. And it gets bigger and bigger until the clam dies or is fished from the sea and the shell is opened."

"It was an accident that caused you to have damaged eyes. It was an accident that caused the little light that you had to go dark. Bad things have happened to you. Bad things have happened to Alice. We can't do anything about your lost eyesight and we can't bring Alice back. I can't tell you any reason for any of these things happening, either to Alice or you. This much I am certain of, in the absence of your eyesight, other things occur in your life, good things. Just like the clam that made changes, so do you. You have developed your other senses to a degree far greater than mine or your mother's. You hear things I can't hear. You smell things your mother can't smell. And your touch. I can't make any sense out of those little Braille dots, and to think you can read from them! You can read in the dark. You don't even need the light."

"You're another pearl, Ruthie, unique, valuable and precious."

I smiled. We were both quiet for a couple of minutes. Then I said,

"Thank you, Papa. I'm pretty lucky to have you and Mama for my parents. I know that. Sometimes, I get to feeling sorry for myself."

"We all do, Pork-chop," he said.

I giggled again at Papa's calling me "Pork-chop". He only calls me that name to tease. So anytime our conversation is serious and he wants to loosen it up and get me to relax he calls me "Pork-chop." It always works.

CHAPTER SEVENTEEN

Flight

With the arrest of the man on the street-car, the students began to relax and returned to a normal school life. The Arkansas Gazette reported the suspect's name was Luther Oddsky, somewhat of a do-nothing, a type of drifter who moved about town, working at odd jobs from time to time. He came from a family of eleven children, all boys, who lived down in the hollar off Little Bayou Road. His folks were share croppers, very poor people who hardly had enough food to feed their family. The neighbor's often reported fights between the boys and between their parents, too. Several of his brothers had arrests' records, most of a minor nature. He didn't. He was 43 years old and had never been married. As I thought about it, that last name struck me as interesting. It's the same as one of the students at the school. Oddsky. *That name isn't very common.*

Grace and I went back to school, ready to plunge ourselves into school work and practice. Oh, the subject of the abduction and murder was still in our everyday conversation. There was so much speculation around town about all aspects of it and some of that spilled over into the school but our teachers never spoke of it after Alice's funeral service. I'm sure they were hoping to bury that trauma in our lives along with Alice's casket.

On Wednesday of that week, I was working on a report for geography, on the mountains of the Eastern world. The map room had temporarily been moved to the conference room, just next to the superintendent's office. There were great bas relief maps set at table height on an inclining angle where I could comfortably reach. I did not understand the extent of the Himalayan Mountains and there in the map room, I could remove the various countries of Napal, India, and China, each cut out into blocks of their own shape and on an accurate scale to that region. The mountain ranges were raised to their relative height. It was there that I could see the shape of the borders. The height of the mountains was much less that I had imagined. So many countries bordered the mountains that when I examined their sizes and noted how small some of those countries were, I got a new image of the total range. It all came into focus for me.

Many times, those maps had given perspective for me, not only to understand my own state but the United States and other countries around the world. I could see their rivers as the indented lines wound through the countryside, or the relationships of their large cities that were marked with a raised dot. The capitals were identified by a raised star. I finished my search and was just walking toward the door leading out to the hall, when my ears caught the sound of a voice I never expected to hear. It was Luther. The Luther on the street car. I stopped transfixed.

The Luther on the street car had been arrested. He was in jail, at least I thought he was in jail.

"Christensen, huh?"

But he was not in jail. That was his voice. I'm sure of it. He was right here at the school, right out in the hall-way outside the map room. The door was open. He'd see me. I threw myself up against the wall at the side of the door opening, turning my face away from the doorway, hoping our uniformed looks would hide me. He was so close. His voice and footsteps grew a little louder before their sound slowly faded down the hall. My fear grew stronger when I acknowledged to myself the owner of the second voice, the voice of the person responding with "I'll call her in for you." It was the school superintendent, Mr. Traegor.

I knew one set of footsteps went down the hall after Luther's voice trailed with "Oh, I know where to find her." The other back footsteps went back into Mr. Traegor's office.

What does this mean? Why was Luther here? Why was he with Mr. Traegor? Why had the police let him go? Or did they? Did Mr. Traegor know him? He must have known him. I didn't understand. I could not have been mistaken about that voice. My heart raced as my body tensed against the wall. Did Luther see me? Maybe he saw my all black school uniform, I rationalized, but didn't see my face. Thank goodness for that! He must have come here looking for me? What did he know? And the greatest question was Mr. Traegor. What was his connection to Luther? Did Mr. Traegor have anything to do with Alice's death?

I couldn't believe what I had heard. Why did Mr. Traegor tell Luther he'd get me? What should I do? Where should I go? I have to think.

I must call Papa, or the police. But the only telephones at the school are in superintendent's office or just outside at his secretary's desk. I can't make a call from the school. That would be like walking into a trap. And I can't go out to the street. Luther may be waiting out in front for me, or someone else, someone I don't even know. They can see me, whoever they are, but I can't see them.

I have to get away from here. My heart pounded and my body tensed like a clothes' line holding a week's wash. *Think, Christensen,* I said to myself. I know I have to get out of here. Home is the only safe place I know. I have to get home.

In a few hours it'll be dark. My black uniform will help me blend into the night but I must avoid the lights at the main entrance. If I can get out the back door and walk across to the edge of the property before getting to the street, I can avoid someone waiting for me there. I'll not chance the street car. But what about the lights? I don't know where the lights are. Maybe I'll be walking right under the lights and not know it. Mama said all the streetcar stops were lit but I don't know where the other lights are, probably not many this far out of town, but when I get into town there are businesses open. Well, at least there will be saloons open. That'll mean lights and people. I heard the Baptist preacher talk about the saloons and about the unsavory characters in and around them. Mama would call that going from the frying pan into the fire.

I can't risk going home by the streets. Well, at least not Main Street. One or two blocks back there are no street-car tracts or business. Perhaps there is more safety there. Papa says to pay attention to my own instincts. I remember when just he and I walked in the woods alone. I was little then and I could easily recognize most of the sounds once I thought about them. I can do this on my own, now. If I move in darkness, the darkness and safety of the back streets, I can go home without a problem. That's what I'll do, the way I'll go.

I set my Braille slate and stylus on a shelf right next to my head, there in the map room. I listened for quiet in the hall. Then I dropped my head down into my chest to hide as much as possible and quickly left through the open doorway, angling across the hall to reach the rear exit. The laundry was the building closest to that exit. I slipped inside it and waited to get my bearings. The door behind me was thrown open. I must have bolted through the roof because I heard, "Sorry to surprise you. Anything I can do for you?" I recognized the voice. It was Manny Lopez, one of the regular laundry workers.

The surprise left me struggling for a deep breath. "I, I, ah, Oh hello, Manny. Ah, no. No, I just needed to stop by to look for that little hooked rug. It was missing when my linens were returned this week."

Manny was staff. He worked under Mr. Traegor. Yet, he was my friend, or I thought so. But can I be sure he won't go right to Traegor? I decided I couldn't afford to trust him.

"Tell you what. Go on over to the mangles and talk with Gertrude. Just follow the carts on the right, on back to the sound of the steam. You'll know when you get close to her. Now, don't get burned. Just follow your ears." His voice trailed as he moved away.

That was fine. Of course, I really didn't need to talk to Gertrude. I just needed time to think. I heard no other voices close by so I followed the laundry carts to the nearest corner and sat on the floor behind one. I heard footsteps come and go and voices that made incidental conversation, over a couple of hours, until it became clear the laundry workers were leaving for the day. The chimes on the great clock next to the conservatory struck four, then five. I sat quietly, continuing

WHAT COLOR IS A BUTTERFLY | 183

to wait and plan. I would stay here until dark and leave the school for home. It wouldn't be safe to leave by the front, or take the streetcar and I knew it was mile to the Arkansas River bridge. I'd never been out the back way, but I'd heard some of the boys talk about that area and I had painted a picture in my head of the area. I could parallel Main street, Louisiana Street, one block to the left or west of the school.

There were fewer homes, and less traffic. Go north. It was only eighteen blocks to the river and then across the river to North Little Rock and home.

When will the sun set? It really was never too relevant to talk about here at the school. At home, it seemed like someone in the family mentioned it almost every day. "Papa should be home before dark." "Go back to sleep, it's still dark," or something like that. I need to figure out when it might be dark. I stood up and reached out to the wall to find a window. There must be a window on this wall. What direction does this wall face? If I could find a western window, I could see if the window was still warm. That would tell my if there was any sun, or daylight now. But it would have to be completely cold before I could venture out. I could only leave by complete darkness. Let's see, now. The morning sun comes into that window next to my bed. That means west is on the opposite side of our room and on the backside of the main building. That would be on the left side of the laundry door I came in. I stood up and followed the carts to the other side of the room, moving toward the wall.

Phew! Those are dirty clothes in that cart, and the next. Also the next. Pushing away laundry carts as I went, I could detect the fresh odor of the cleansing soap, and reaching over tables there were the shelves of clean laundry. I found the first window. It was cold. I looked for another. These shelves had clean towels stacked on them. This window was cold. What if the sun never reached this window? It'd be cold all day. I looked for a third window, past another row of shelves, this time full of blankets. Aha! It was slightly warm. There still must be some sun on that one window, or if it is already dark, it hasn't been dark long. I must wait a little while longer.

I sat down on a tiny bench or stepping stool that was set out a little from the wall. I pushed it close to the wall so my back rested against it. I took a deep breath. *"What am I doing? What am I doing?"* I reconsidered. *"Am I doing the right thing? But what are my choices? I have none. Papa always said I could depend on my own senses, my own head. Move slowly and think. This is the time if there ever was a time. I must get away from here."*

Maybe, it was thirty minutes later that I rechecked the warm window. It was cold, as cold as the other two. Now is the time. But the temperature of the laundry was now considerably cooler than when I came in. I should have a coat or sweater.

I checked the shelves again, from top to bottom. I pulled down one of the cotton blankets, wrapped it around my shoulders and sure enough, I let my nose lead me to the odor of kerosene. The wool blankets were cleaned with that smelly stuff and I need one of those for these chilly evenings. Besides the wood blankets on our beds were dark, "a practical gray," Mama had said. It would help me be as inconspicuous as possible.

As I reached the outside door of the laundry, I paused to wrap a dark one over my head and shoulders like mama sometimes did with a shawl. I turned the door handle. The door didn't budge. It was locked. I tried one last time and it moved. One last push and it thrust open. Quickly, I stepped out and closed the door behind me and started walking down the walk. It was supper time. I could smell the beef stew with onions and celery. Cookie usually served it with fresh biscuits. My urgency to get out of a scary situation way prevented me from thinking much about being hungry. The school was quiet, so everyone must be in for supper.

At the end of the concrete walk, the dirt path began. In another forty or fifty steps, the path turned into the road that I recognized was the one that crossed the grounds, down to the lower end past the smelly compost pile where I had never been. I was sure I couldn't be seen from awayone waiting for me on the street in front of the school. I could hear a dog in the distance. There were no dogs at the school. I wondered who and where he belonged. A gentle breeze caused a slight rustle of leaves high above the road. There were no voices, no other noises. I was alone.

*   *   *

We were already asleep, when the telephone rang. This was not unusual for doctors. Night calls were not an everyday occurrence but they came frequently enough that when the phone rang, neither Peter nor I was the least bit surprised. The call was for Peter, all right, but as soon as I heard his voice respond to the caller I sat upright in bed.

"Why have you not called earlier?" his voice showed concern. "What time is it, now?" There was a delay for the caller to answer before he responded.

"Have you called the police?" Another delay. And then he snapped. "For God's sake, man, why not?"

This call was not a call for a doctor. I threw back the covers and stood up. That kind of language was not used by my mild mannered husband. Who was missing? Was it one of our girls? I thought I had heard Esther come in. Inger had not been out. She'd been at home all evening. It couldn't have been Ruth. Or could it? Oh no, was it Ruth? Ruth was at the school. She couldn't have been missing?

"Who is it?" I asked Peter.

He looked up at me and didn't answer. He turned to look down to the floor and he slowly shook his head. I waited silently as Peter covered his remaining ear, straining to hear what the caller was saying, straining to shut out my voice. I jumped out of bed and pulled the light chain. When he hung up the phone, he lowly turned to meet my eyes.

Who doesn't know where she is? Is it Ruth? She's at school of course. Certainly she's there. You took her there yourself last Sunday night," I stated fact.

"Listen to me, Mary. Ruth is missing. She was at classes all day but did not appear for her organ lesson at 4 o'clock, missed dinner last night and has not been seen since."

"That's not possible," I refused to believe what I was hearing. "Tell me this is a mis . . ." Peter stopped me.

"Listen to me. Ruth is missing from the school. Believe me. If she were there, we would not have gotten the call. Be quiet for a moment and let me think."

My mind was racing, but I bit my lip and remained silent as I reached deep into my lungs for a full breath. Peter began to pace the room, arms stretched behind him. I thought about what could have happened. She was inside the school and then suddenly she was not there. Organized classes are already over before 4 o'clock. The school rather disperses for yard activity, or library work or practice in the conservatory. Students use that time for shop work or craft activities. There are lots of people around.

"Someone must know something," I broke into Peter's words.

"When was she last seen? And who called?"

"She left her elocution class about 3:30 and that instructor didn't know where she was going from there. They've only talked with her teachers and the girls who were her closest friends. None of them know anything," Peter was animated.

"I can't accept his excuse for not calling the police." Peter was in his own thoughts and I couldn't stand him ignoring me. I wanted to shake him when he answered me, very slowly and deliberately.

"Traegor. It was Traegor who called."

"Why not? What was his excuse? For not calling the police, I mean?" I asked.

He said, "He thought Ruth might have stayed away with her boy friend. She has no boy friend . . . that is no serious boy friend. I know my daughter and she would not miss her piano lesson. Maybe some of his charges might be out with a boy friend but Ruth! Not Ruth. He's lying. Traegor is not telling the truth. I need to know why? I'm calling Chief Amos myself right now," he said.

"It's almost five o'clock in the morning," I announced.

"I don't care what time it is. I'm getting him out of bed," Peter was adamant, already removing the receiver from the wall phone and turned the crank with his right hand.

"Get me Chief Amos's home. Right aw . . . Oh, Hello, Myrtle. Sorry I didn't say anything to you. This is an emergency. Please ring up the Chief."

The Chief answered immediately, like he was expecting a call. The conversation with Chief Amos was long, miserably long since I could only hear one side of it and desperately needed to hear the answers. Then Peter said, "I'm coming, too?"

"Where?" I asked. "Where are you going?"

Peter's eyebrows furrowed as he quietly waited for the chief to finish speaking. The wait seemed like an eternity. His voice lowered as he began to speak.

"I guess you're right. All right, I'll stay right here. But you'll keep me informed, won't you? Call me as soon as you have any information at all."

He replaced the receiver on the 'U' shaped holder on the left side of the telephone box that hung in the hall and turned to me.

"Tell me. Tell me everything." I could not keep still. His eyes met mine and he began.

"It seems that Traegor called the station just after he called us. Chief Amos had just been called by his man at the station house and he's on his way to the school, now. But, he also told me that he had released the suspect in Alice's murder. He checked his alibi and had no basis for holding him any longer. That man's out on the street."

I gasped as I put my hands on my face. He quickly continued.

"Now, Mary, that man may not be involved with Alice at all. Just because he attempted to detain Ruth doesn't make him a murderer. Amos also said he didn't think he was very bright, either. I think we need to set that Luther person back into our minds until we know something more about him. Don't let your imagination carry you into something that may not be so."

He began to dress and I went to the kitchen to make coffee. We had an early breakfast that morning. Peter took forever shaving. He was just waited around for the Chief to call. When he didn't call, Peter was simply too edgy to sit and wait so he left for the School for the Blind to get what information he could.

He wouldn't let me go with him. "You need to stay here with the telephone," he said. "Chief Amos says someone needs to remain here at all times."

By the time he arrived at the school, it was almost 6 a.m. Of course, the news of Ruth's disappearance was all over the school by now. The house mother had awakened all her closest friends during the night to get any information about her from them. Most people didn't think too much about her missing dinner. They talked of it but said she might be practicing late, or studying. But she didn't usually miss meals. This is exactly the beginning sequence of events when Alice disappeared. This was foremost in the kids' minds.

Several had come forth with bits and pieces of information. The outside workers were arriving, those who worked at the farm and the grounds, and the laundry. The yard superintendent had already been called in by Mr. Traegor. He knew nothing and agreed to send in his people when they arrived for work.

Manny Lopez was just coming down the walk. "Not today," he answered to the question about seeing Ruth. "I just got here." He hesitated, "wait a minute. Yesterday afternoon? Yeah, she was in the laundry about four o'clock. And, funny thing, she had asked about her little rug and I sent her over to the mangle. I didn't think anything about it. I didn't see her after that."

Not all of the laundry staff was there. The man who operated the big ironing machine called in sick. He wasn't there to question.

Someone else had found a Braille slate and stylus with the name "Ruth C" scratched into them. Those belonged to Ruth Christensen. They were found in the map room that was temporarily located right next to Traegor's office. Peter was not allowed to speak with Traegor at the time. Nor could he talk with Chief Amos. He was told that Chief Amos was in Traegor's office.

CHAPTER EIGHTEEN

Pooch

The October night was breezy, not the biting wind of the previous week, but still it was chilly. I'm so glad to have the two blankets from the laundry. Stopping momentarily to raise the outer blanket up higher on my neck, I continued walking through the silence rather quickly. The road had a gentle but continuous drop as it stretched further away from the buildings I'd long known to be "the school." There were no steps back here to surprise a sightless child. I knew that in all the years the school cared for the children there would be little risk from sudden steps or otherwise unexpected changes in the path.

Papa had talked about the creeks that snaked through the countryside that feed into the Arkansas River. The summer heat usually dried up those creeks, and this year had been a particularly hot and dry July and August. The route close to the dry creeks would lead me to the river, they were off the roads, out of sight from anyone out looking for me. I paid attention to each change in direction as I walked the distance away from the school, always projecting the direction of the river and the foot-bridge across that would ultimately take me home to safety.

Before traveling alone on the street cars to school, Papa had pointed out to me that the city streets were laid out on a grid, neatly and evenly with no curves in the street-car lines. I knew that I needed to go north from the school in order to reach the river, the reverse of my travel from North Little Rock to the school. In the dozens of times I'd ridden that street-car, I knew every street crossing and stop, every lurch and wobble of the cars, gentle movement that came from an unevenness in the tract, as opposed to the full weight-shift in the car as the street-car made its turn toward the station house just after crossing the river. When we rode over from home in Papa's buggy, the road was straight all the way to the station house and then on to the school. In my mind, I reconfirmed which direction was south or north when I thought of the direction of the sun's warmth coming into the windows of the street-car. I could position the sun not only from the time I boarded the car just a block from Papa's office, but as we crossed the river and changed cars to go out to the school. When I reversed directions and went from the school to go home, the sun was on my left cheek. If I sat on the other side of the car on the way home, there was no warm sun. I was sure of that.

Thinking about the street-car after it left the station to cross the river to Arjenta, we made a 90 degree turn to the left in less than a minute. In a few blocks the hollow sound of the open space beneath the car tracks announced we were over the river. That meant the station was west, just a little west of the bridge home. However, when Papa drove me in his buggy he had to take a different bridge than the one for street-cars. Since this time, I'd be going the other direction, I needed only to turn the directions around in my mind. The second bridge was used for people walking, or for wagons and buggies. It was called the "free bridge" because there was no charge. We rode farther east to get to that bridge, not much farther east. Maybe it was about a couple of blocks to the other bridge. That didn't really matter because that bridge was on the same street as Papa's office, a direct line to his office. I had to get to that bridge.

I had this all organized in my long wait in the laundry. It would be the first time in my life I had traveled along the river alone, any river. Papa used to play a game with me as a child when our family went fishing. He'd send me on ahead so I could find my way from his fishing spot back to the picnic pallet or the buggy, but he was always back there keeping an eye on me. I knew then I'd be stopped if I made the wrong turn. There would be no one to stop me this time. I'll just be me, but that's as easy as licking the cake frosting bowl. I'm not afraid, at least not afraid of getting lost, but Luther or who else might be looking for me is another matter.

The road began to turn south. No, No. Wrong way! I need to go the other direction. I stopped. I must go north to get to the river but there must be a foot-trail in the opposite direction, just like the road. Usually, this distance to town there is a path along the edge of the creek. This was in a clearing of sorts because I passed the last tree about twenty steps back. I walked to the road's edge, easily detectable by the softer ground. Years of wagon wheels had hardened the main path of the road. The outer edges were softer and in the springtime, those areas sprouted fresh weeds. Now the grasses were dry and discouraged for they crunched like soft straw under my feet.

Here it is! Here's a change in the road's edge, but let's see now. Is this a real trail? I patted the surface with the ball of my foot, looking for the width of the hardened path. It would be slightly indented, too. I stretched my foot over. The ground was hard for about 15 or 18 inches before the path's edge identified itself with the raised edge of dry weeds, shaved to a stubble from months of foot traffic.

There it is! That's a good sized path. I'll bet this was not just a foot-trail. I'll bet this is used for horses, probably other farm animals, too.

I thought about the difference in the sounds made by my own footsteps and what those meant. The knocking noise that I heard when my heels hit the wooden walks outside Papa's office changed when I came to the end of the block, where the dirt and mud of the road's edge began. A long time ago, I learned that when I heard that sound I could expect a slight drop down in the city's walks, down to the road to be crossed. When I was a younger I related it to the "thickness" of the sound, like the difference in the knock on the big door at the church and the small cabinet doors at home. Papa said when the thickness of the wood in the doors and the surface underneath was reduced, so was the sound. Now I know it is really an echo.

Grace Davenport told me once that the Indians in Oklahoma traveled by those echoes. "The Indians survive by tracking their food. At times their lives depend on tracking their own predators. They were so good because they paid attention to every tiny noise, noises so small that most of us never even hear them. We all are capable of hearing them but only the Indians seem to pay attention to them."

More than the Indians listen to the echoes. I do. Walking on the hard ground sounds very different from the hard wood. Hard wood resting on a surface makes a different noise than a wooden plank with open space beneath. Footsteps on grass is much different still. And even then, if the grass has brittle twigs or some dry edges, that's a dead giveaway of movement. Few footsteps are in complete silence. With my shoes on, I can still get an echo from each surface and those sounds help guide me.

I need a pole or big stick to help sound out the path. Maybe under that last tree is a broken limb.

I retraced my steps to the tree I had just passed. Walking under its branches, I looked for the right sized limb, not too old to be so brittle to crumble on contact and not too fresh to bend into uselessness when it touched the ground. I almost tripped when my toe caught on one downed branch, but I gently sat down by shifting my weight backwards, catching myself with my right hand. There it was, right under my hand. It was the perfect pole after I removed some of the smaller side branches.

I returned to the newly discovered path, I tested my new walking stick, moving it ahead of me to probe in a wide arc. There were bushes along side the path and in a short distance, I was aware of many trees. The trees always lined the creeks, but I heard no water. That was good. I wanted a dry creek bed.

Perhaps it was two, maybe three hours, that I walked before I heard another barking dog. He seemed to be getting closer very fast. I figured he must be moving toward me because his barking got louder quickly and then he snarled. He was upon me.

I stopped. I didn't dare move. It was like he was challenging me to cross his land, to intrude into his space, to invade his protectorship. I stood transfixed. He stayed put, also. He stopped his growl. He was testing me, I knew.

"Hello," I said softly. "Nice, doggy." I began to talk to him as I stood perfectly still. I shifted my walking pole and he moved, I'm sure, but he no longer growled.

"Is it all right if I walk on?" I asked, knowing I wouldn't get an answer, but relaxing a bit when the movement of my pole aroused no alarm in him.

Very small steps, at first, I tested him. I got no reaction, so I lengthened them five, then six steps. I could hear his soft foot pads when he crunched a brittle twig beneath him. He was following me. I stopped and called out to him.

"Come, pooch. Come on up so I can pet you. We can be friends, you and me," I said. I put one hand out through the opening between my blanket wrap. I could sense he was moving closer, very slowly, checking on me, testing, but he wasn't a threat, I was sure. He didn't walk up to my hand. I extended it a little further and brushed his wet nose.

"Oh, there you are. Come let me see how big you are and let's see, now." He stood still and I was the one to move toward him. "Can I guess what kind of dog you are? You're larger than a collie and about the height and length of the hunting dogs I've seen, the coon-dogs. But your hair is too long for any of the hunting dogs I've ever seen. "I'll bet you're a police dog. Are you a police dog?"

I knew his tail was wagging by the muscle action at the base of his spine. I knew we were now friends.

"Well, come on. Friends walk together and we're in this together, just you and me," I said. I began walking again and Pooch followed behind me, then ahead of me and back along side me, as if he was my escort, my guard. He was also my company. In the dark of night his eyes could see more than mine and that might be useful to me. He was someone or something I could talk to and he had his own way of answering me, a break in his panting, a change in his breathing, where he walked.

Walking on for another 15 or 20 minutes I sensed a clearing. It was directly in front of me. I stopped abruptly and listened to the sounds around me. "What 's out there, Pooch?" I reached along side my right leg where I sensed his presence. I patted his head and Pooch made a little whining noise. There was a little more wind on my face and no sound of crickets chirping ahead. Their calls were with me, on the right and left of my path. Why not in front of me? Have we reached the creek? I moved ahead very slowly, extending my pole to the front as far out as possible. Sure enough there was a drop in my path. I moved my stick out to see if I could find an edge beyond and on the sides. My stick found a slanted earth angling downward. I sat down to probe for the ground in front of me, to see how deep my pole went.

I whistled. The sound returned to me, an echo, a slightly hollow sound. I had reached the creek, a very quiet creek. It's dry, I think. At least there's not enough water for movement. This was the right path to the creek but I didn't think I should try it because the dept was in question. Even though along side the creek would be the safest route for me I was uneasy about it and pushed the ground on both sides of my body to rise and find another direction. I was dangling my legs over the bank, when the bank gave way and I tumbled down to the bottom.

I came to rest against a stone. A warm, wet liquid rolled down my right temple. Oh, my head! Pooch was right there, nosing my face and licking my cheek. I lay still, trying to think of what happened. My head cleared and I started to sit up, dabbing my forehead with the cotton blanket. "I guess I fell, huh, Pooch?"

Supporting myself with my left land, I pushed myself up. The pain in my wrist was excruciating and I dropped back to the ground. I rolled over to my back, stretching out my left hand, gasping from the pain. *Maybe I broke it. Oh-o-o! But I can't stay here. I've got to get home.*

Pooch was right there with his sympathetic wet nose and drooling on my face. I reached over to touch his back fur and stroke him. I patted his head and gently rubbed his head between his ears. "I'm so glad you're with me, Pooch." His warm body was so welcome since my blankets were on the ground, somewhere. The creek bed is covered with rocks, smooth and rounded, and warm, still warm from the day's sun.

That's why the crickets aren't in this area. They like the moisture of the grass up along the trail and these hot rocks dry out the earth too much.

It's been harder to keep my footing on this uneven earth. I'd be better off back on the path. Also, I know the way back up at this point. Another place might be harder to climb out of. I've got to get back to my path above. That trail continued on up to the north and I must focus on that direction. Rolling over to my right side, I jimmied into position to rise onto my knees and right arm. I pushed myself up holding my painful left arm close to my body for protection. It was hard to avoid using my left arm. I stooped to find my pole and blankets. I didn't find the pole so I had to at least try to manage without it. I swung the blankets up to the shelf of earth that I dropped off originally. I could find another pole up top, hopefully. Pooch was already up there, facing me and panting as if to give me encouragement. Then I struggled, twisting and writhing to get a hold of any growth to help hoist my body up to the shelf. I dug my toes into the slanted earth and pushed with my feet and pulled on a small tree. I made it back up to the shelf.

"Thanks Pooch. We both made it, didn't we?"

My wrist was now throbbing and I was cold. I had to get the blankets around me and hold them by my painful arm. I had bumped my bad arm twice in the process and reached over with my good arm to stroke the area of greatest pain. It was warm down by the wrist, and that's where it hurt the most. "I hope it's not broken. Maybe it's sprained," I said to the pooch.

The path back toward the school was the first trail I came to. I could tell by the gradual change to my right for just three steps before the path got wider and deeper. I recognized it. Turning my body back to generally face the direction I knew I needed to go, I searched with my foot for the path leading parallel to the creek, not down to it. It was there, on the other side of the fork. Keeper my directional perspective was crucial. Now more than ever, I needed a staff or probe. Leaving the path for a moment and facing away from the creek, I again searched for another big stick, brushing Pooch's fur or nose in the process. It had to be a tall one. A limb brushed my cheek from overhead. I stopped to break it off for use and then thought again. A fresh branch would be too flexible and it must be dry enough to be stiff. I kicked around with my foot and picked up the first one I came to for better examination. The first one was pretty brittle but if I didn't put too much weight on it I could manage with that one. No better one was within my reach so I decided to move ahead with this stick. It'll have to do.

For over two or three hours, I walked. The sounds of the barking dog had gotten a little closer before it faded off as I evidently distanced myself from him. I had to get my mind off the pain in my wrist. I forced my thoughts to other things, happy things, good thoughts. Sometimes, I tried to sing, softly, just enough to hear the sound of my voice. It was then a little like I was someone besides Pooch. I giggled to myself when I re-thought that. Except for the pouch, how more alone could I get.

The path wound its way gently back and forth, in and around trees, but always to the northerly direction I needed to go. The crickets talked to me as their voices pointed out my path. One kind of cricket had a series of clattering, something like the rattle of a rattle-snake, but not exactly and much quieter. The one with two syllables on the same pitch was the cricket that interested me any time the path turns.

"Thank you, little crickets," I laughed when I said it.

"Who-o-o!" I must have jumped a foot into the air.

"That's an owl," I said aloud. Then I began to giggle again. "I should be afraid of an owl. Ha!" I resumed my walk, laughing at myself and my panic at what was probably a very small owl, certainly a harmless bird. I began to imitate the owl's call and think about the pitch of his voice. It was deeper that the crickets. *But that's logical because it's so much larger than the crickets. Naturally the larger the vocal chords, the deeper the pitch of the voice,"* I reasoned with myself. I continued to walk.

My pain demanded some attention. I raised my arm and realized the wrist held at shoulder height felt better so it remained high.

I no longer could hear the occasional sound of the street-cars moving about in the distance. *Was it because I was too far from them?* I pondered that question. *Do any of the cars run all night? It must be getting late. I wonder what time it is?*

"Whew, I'm tired. It's getting colder, too." I stopped to rewrap my slipping blankets and one fell to the ground. I reached down to pick it up and in the process, dropped the other one. Down on my knees to search for the other blanket and its four corners. I just sat down onto the cotton blanket. It felt good to get off my feet for a minute and so I just stretched out, thinking I would relax for just a few minutes. I leaned back, rolled over onto my side, curling up in a ball and covered myself with the heavier, wool blanket.

I must have dropped off to sleep and when I stirred thought about how warm and toasty it was there on the ground, warmer on one side than the other. I startled, tensed and hesitated, listening intently. I could hear it yawning and then shaking. "It's the pooch."

"Oh, pooch, you're still here? You'll keep me warm, won't you? I think you and I are pals, aren't we? Huh?" He was still as if listening to my questions.

"'You going to travel all the way with me? Well, let's get going. I've got to get home before Mama and Papa know I left the school. "They'll be worried sick if they find out I'm not at school."

I sat up and patted the dog for just a minute. Then checking to find both blankets, I stood up and first put the cotton blanket over my shoulders and head. Shielding my hurting wrist as much as possible I then wrapped the wool blanket around my shoulders. My feet stepped on one of the blankets on my first step so I hoisted it a little higher. I knew I had to get moving to warm up. I found my walking stick and trudged ahead.

"Listen to my cricket friends, pooch," I said. "I wonder what's going on with them? Their voices have changed." That is, their pitch had lowered, lower than those around the school. Some of the crickets around the school were at high "C". I don't hear anything higher that "B" natural now. Maybe it's a different kind a cricket that a cicada. I discounted that theory when I rationalized that the calls were identical to those around me now. When they appeared in front of me, I knew the path was turning. I probed with both the pole and my foot until I found the trail. In just a minute or so the trail turned into a larger trail heading again in what I was sure to be a northerly direction.

It was only occasionally now that I smelled the manure of the barnyards. The houses seem closer together, too. I've left the small farms around the school and I'm coming closer to town. Many families had a horse to pull their buggies and many raised their own chickens. Some had cows for the milk and butter. When the houses are closer together I'm getting into town.

After walking for another half hour or so, I came to a road. It intersected my path like the arm of a cross. The ground's surface changed and I stopped when I sensed the open space of a roadway on both my right and my left. "It's so very quiet, no sounds in either side. I thought I heard a horse make that snorting noise, like he had some dust or something in his nose. In the distance ahead of me, across the road, the crickets voice pitch was lower.

"Why?" I thought. "What's the difference in those crickets and the ones back there?"

I crossed the road but I couldn't find the path. Walking along the road to the left for 15 or 20 feet and searching with my pole and my feet, I found no path. Reversing directions and returning to the original point I probed to the right, in the direction I need to go anyway. I found it, a very narrow path and winding slightly to the right. "Great, that'll go to the free bridge!" I thought. "That's where I need to go."

Then I heard a splash and the gurgling sound of the dog drinking water. Pooch seemed lower than me, maybe in a hole. I stopped in my path. He must have looked up because I heard the drinking stop and water dripping down to the water below him.

"Did he find a pond? Was it a drinking trough for livestock?"

I walked forward, slowly probing with my stick, listening to the echoes of my steps, of my pole. Trees were on both sides of me but dead ahead was open space.

I've reached the river. It's moving so gently it hardly makes a sound. That's why the cricket voices are lower. It's because it's cooler on the river. Their voices are always lower in the colder weather. I'm at the river, the Arkansas River. "I'm halfway home, pooch. Come on this way. We have to find the bridge across the river."

CHAPTER NINETEEN

Home

"Come on, Pooch. You and I are back-tracking to the road. That's the road to town, I'm sure and town's the route home. Let's go."

I turned to the road and Pooch followed soon brushing my leg as he passed me and led the way. We turned what I thought to be east, walking on the hard surface of the road. Within five minutes, I heard horses' hooves, that is, four hooves which meant one horse. He's pulling a wagon of metal cans, full cans by the sound, sturdy rather than the many clinking rattles of the empty cans. They were full, probably full of milk. *Sure, this was the time for milk delivery.* I moved off the road to the grassy area. *The milk wagon will be Okay. I can hail him down and get him to take me home. I'll just wave to him and he'll stop.*

He was close enough now so I could hear the driver talking. He wasn't alone. I moved to the edge of the road. Just as the wagon came even with me, I waived knowing he would stop. I could hear a child's voice speaking also. He wasn't slowing down.

I called out as the wagon passed me. "Stop! Hey!"

The wagon continued. He didn't stop. *Why didn't he stop?*

Maybe he couldn't see me. They must have lanterns on the milk wagons. I think all wagons carry kerosene lanterns but I don't really know. Then I remembered my uniform. *It's dark and my blankets are dark also. The people on the wagon were talking and maybe not paying attention. They probably don't expect to run across a hitchhiker at this time of the morning.*

"Well Pooch, we missed that one. Let's keep going on our own."

The hard surface of the road made for easier walking. There was more activity now. The morning was starting in a quiet hum, with a barking dog in the distance, a rooster crowing and a slammed door here and there. I could hear a couple of men's voices out ahead of me. From the smell of dried grass or hay, I gathered I was approaching a feed store or granary. They may open early for the farm trade.

I stopped to listen to the men talking about their families and their children. I liked what I heard, the humor and the gentleness of their voices. "*These are good men*", I thought.

"'You still with me, Pooch?" He was quiet but I knew he was close by when I heard his panting. "Come on, let's stop here."

I called out. "Hello! You there, hello!"

Silence. I called out again.

"'Mornin'," came the answer.

"I need some help, please," I said. He was walking toward me because his voice was getting louder.

"Where did you come from, Miss? 'You have a horse around here somewheres?"

"No, I've run away from my school. I thought I was in danger and I need to get to my home in Arjenta. Would you please call my parents to come get me?"

"No schools are open this early, Miss. 'Ya kiddin us?"

"No. I'm serious, sir. I've been out all night trying to get home."

"Home from where? A party?"

"The School for the Blind."

One of the men began to laugh, "Sure you came from the school like my name's Abraham Lincoln. That school's way far away and you couldn't have walked from there, at least not alone like you are.

"Please sir, please telephone my parents, number 396. My father will come for me if you just let him know where I am. I'm very tired and I want to go home."

"Do you know your address?" Not waiting for my answer, he said.

"Tell you what. I'll do better and get the buggy out and take you home myself.

I had not a moment's hesitation. I trusted this man. "I can tell you how to get there. Can we get started?"

"I'll need to get my wagon hitched. You just wait here with your dog. It'll just take a minute."

Going out the yard opening, I said, "Washington Street. In Arjenta." Pooch sat on the bench between us.

He said very little as we went into the center of town, turned left and over the bridge and called out to the old man who guarded the bridge. "Mornin' Baxter."

He knew to take it slow when crossing that bridge and that Baxter's house was on the Arjenta side of the river. When we stopped in front of our house, the driver came over to help me down from the wagon but I already had one foot on the wheel. I'd ridden on wagons many times before. I didn't need any help. He walked up to the house with me. I knew he doubted my story from beginning to end. *He probably took me home so he could confront my lying, or so he thought.*

I walked right in the front door, through to Mama's kitchen. My driver told Mama it was impossible for me to come that far, my being blind "and all." But Mama was in no mood to prove anything to this man. She tried to be gracious. She thanked him for bringing me home, telling him how thankful she was that I was safe.

"I'll cut you a piece of fresh apple pie for your lunch." Then she showed him back to the front door."

I told Mama as much as I could while I ate a cold drumstick and drank a cup of warm milk, and Mama cleaned and dressed my wrist. Then she set a wash pan full of warm water with a bar of soap and washcloth in it so I could wash my face and hands as she cleaned my forehead. Home never felt so good and I was asleep almost before my head hit the pillow. To Mama and Papa the most important thing was that I was home. I was safe.

It was almost noon by the time I woke up. I had forgotten the pooch but he stayed right with me for he was at the foot of my bed when I woke up. Mama was still in the kitchen when I went downstairs.

Papa'd left instructions that he was to be called as soon as I woke up. But he always came home for his noon meal and it was about that time.

Papa first looked at my wrist and directed Mama on how to treat it as I began telling Papa about the events of the day before. Then he explained that Chief Amos released Luther.

"Why? How could he?" I yelled in fear and disbelief. "He had come to get me," mentally recalling the overheard conversation and my escape to the laundry.

"Because Luther proved to him that he could not have been involved with Alice's disappearance because he was on the way to Memphis at that time. His alibi was verified by one of his men.

"But Papa, I heard him. I heard him say he had to find me."

Papa slowly began to speak. "It's pretty threatening to many of you young ladies, just knowing of the disappearance of one of your own classmates. That pushes alarms off in the parents and the teachers, too, who take care of all of you. However, it's very important that all of us relax enough to clear our heads and not jump to conclusions too fast. What did Luther mean when he said he'd find you? That doesn't mean he's going to hurt you? However, given the threats you all felt after Alice we were certainly wise to be cautious. On the other hand we certainly don't want to accuse anyone who is completely free of any connection to Alice's disappearance."

Chief Amos and I have discussed that at length. The Chief concluded that Luther's social graces were awkward and clumsy, being raised in the country with all the boisterous boys around. He wasn't overly bright and he simply didn't know how to act around young women. Papa said Luther was probably trying to be helpful but he was so different from the other friends of mine. In addition, according to the chief, his neighbors relayed Luther's show of kindness when their dog was injured. His ability to commit a violent act was in serious doubt.

There were several puzzling details of Alice's death. The main question was how did she die? If she wasn't stabbed, shot or strangled, then how? There were several bruises around her nose and mouth but none on her neck. And no object was found in her throat or mouth.

Another question was how did she get to the ditch? The area where Alice's body was found was over two miles from the school. She was fully clothed although the rear seam on her left arm-shoulder was ripped. Several finger-nails on both hands had been broken.

Alice had been found by a couple of teenaged boys returning home from an early morning coon hunt. When they walked the rail-road tracks going out for the hunt, they noticed the decaying odor and their coon-dog wandered from them temporarily. They paid no notice because rodents and small animals are killed on the road often. Of course, it was dark when they went out and the lights on their caps were directed down the tracks to where they wanted to go.

When they returned, the sun was up and they noticed a clump of dark rags down below the elevated railroad tracks. Then when they noticed the red hair, they looked more closely and found Alice. That spot was only about 15 feet off the road. That was a pretty often used road that wound out from town through the countryside. There were many small farms out that way, west of the city. Some were milk producers, others raised pigs or chickens. Most people out in the country raised crops mainly for their own use and sold what they didn't eat, or didn't need, or they canned it for the winter. Everyone out there had smoke houses where they could salt and cure their pork, where they made their sausage. They traveled the road often for runs into town for supplies. This was country so all pretty well knew their neighbors. They were all nice people who went to church on Sundays and respected the Sabbath. Large families were pretty typical of these folks, the more children there were meant more hands to work the fields or other chores. Oh, some of the boys got a little rowdy at times, like all boys are prone to do sometime. Those families, further down, toward the hollows do more cat fishing than crop raising. Those who do the fishing start before dawn so they can have the fresh fish on the street by 10 o'clock in the morning. Then as soon as all the fish was sold the boys are out on their own. They seem to have more free time than those who work the fields.

Alice's mother told the Chief that Alice was in good health except for an occasional attack of asthma. Long ago she learned that she couldn't eat pecans because pecans caused a violent asthmatic reaction. So she stayed away from pecans and never had anymore trouble with asthma.

It was several weeks later that the Gazette announced the arrest of two of the other Oddsky boys. The charge was manslaughter in Alice's death. It seems that when Alice's brother left her off that last day, the Gazette reported that the Oddsky boys had just left the school after dropping off their younger brother, Ivan. Both the older brothers had sniffed cocaine before arriving at the school. On seeing Alice approaching the school they thought they'd have a little fun with her so they caught up with Alice and told her that her brother had just had an accident. He had just left her but she needed to get to her brother. They steered her down a dirt path on the other side of the school. Then when no one else was in sight one of the boys said he wanted to kiss her and put his arms around her. She resisted and began yelling. One of the boys held her shoulders and the other covered her mouth. Unfortunately that amount of fear and trauma caused an asthmatic reaction and she stopped breathing. Her body went limp and she died right then and there.

They left her in the foot high grass and went home for the wagon. The three had time to decide what to do on the return home. They decided on the dump spot as they were returning to the school at twilight, just off the very road they were on. The road was both away from the school and almost a mile from their home and not heavily traveled.

It was dark by the time they got back to the school. It was most people's supper time and no one was around. One of the boys became a look-out for the other two as they lifted Alice's body into the wagon and covered her with a horse blanket they had brought with them. When they got to the pre-planned spot they dumped her body in the low spot between the railroad tracks and the road home.

"Oh, Papa, I feel so much better just knowing who killed Alice. I feel safer now. Would it have happened if cocaine were not in the equation?" Papa said probably not. But who knows? That family was often referred to as "poor white trash". Courteousness was unknown to that crowd and consideration for others was "too sissy." It was for women only, not the tough males in their crowd.

Mama said apparently Mrs. Oddsky had more children than she could handle or perhaps she didn't have the moral or physical stamina to control the boys. Maybe she simply didn't know how to be a mother.

Papa talked to me about my "escape" from the school that afternoon and said that he was proud of me for using my head to travel through the back country like I did. He said that I had done a very dangerous thing to leave like I did, suddenly, and that there must have been someone at the school for me to go to for help. He and Mama were worried sick about me. The school was very concerned but all in all he said he might have done the same thing I did.

"Couldn't you have trusted the nurse? Miss Minnie is her name, isn't it?" Mama asked.

"Oh, yes." I said, but remember both Mr. Traegor and Luther were out in the halls looking for me. They can see me from a distance and I could only recognize Luther if I'm close enough to get a whiff of his body odor or hear his voice. That may be too late unless someone else is there to help me, and Miss Minnie is too far away from the map room to chance getting to her without being spotted by Luther or Mr. Traegor."

I turned to face Papa. "I was at a disadvantage, Papa."

Papa agreed and said nothing else.

After that the school settled back into a routine adjusting only slightly when the state's trustees replaced Mr. Traegor. His wife moved out of the house at the school and no one heard from them again.

Marriage

The last year of school was filled with plans for the future for us all. It was the last time to do our best for the school, too. The trades classes spent the year preparing all kinds of products to show the public and sell, brooms of all types and sizes, rugs, mattresses and handwork. Certainly we all wanted to show our parents. Grace Davenport and I both had several compositions that were performed in concert by the school choir or selected instrumentalist students. Those works were at risk of being lost for future performances by sighted person because of my inability to create a score on paper. Sighted persons needed to be able to READ a score in order to learn it. My joy of writing was therefore somewhat diminished knowing of that limitation. I did copy my works in Braille and New York Point for blind musicians. On several occasions Mrs. Trebing would score my compositions for which I have been forever grateful.

The greatest thrill for most composers was hearing their compositions in concert. In my opinion the ultimate of acceptance is knowing that other musicians want to study and prepare my work for an audience to hear. Professor Trebing requested the ladies' choir at the school to perform my humorous arrangement called "Hey, Diddle, Diddle". It was written in four part harmony and in some places six part harmony. Grace requested that for recital we play my work for organ and piano in classical style. An outsider asked that my arrangement of a hymn be played for her husband's funeral service. People had to hear my compositions first to be aware of the work and more and more the newspapers would report on my compositions. Others became interested in my performing them.

There were great parties for my graduation class and after that my classmates scattered. All left immediately for their homes wherever they were. For the summer Grace Davenport got a job playing organ for a large church in Kansas City and then in the fall entered the University of Oklahoma as a music major. She graduated in only one year due to the quality of the music education she received under Professor Trebing. Then when she graduated from OU she got a contract teaching pipe organ and band in the Oklahoma School for the Blind in Muskogee. We kept in touch by writing each other in Braille.

Several other students went to other colleges, two entered into business, one was a brilliant merchant in the coal supply business, one sold insurance and another opened a piano store in Beaumont, Texas to sell new pianos and tune and repair older ones.

Later in the life of the insurance person, Jim Porter, he learned to drive a car even though he was legally blind. At that time a driver license was not required in the state. One day when he about 60 year old at the time he backed down his driveway to the street that just happened to be on the same street as his office. It was a small town and everyone in town knew old Jim was "blind", so when a car came down the middle of main street with the horn honking frantically the townspeople knew it was the blind man and got out of his way. But as luck sometime goes, one morning a young soldier and his bride were driving through town unaware of the peculiarities of this charming town and its blind citizen. Their car collided with old Jim. After the investigation by the single local policeman, the soldier was heard to say "Who's going to believe me when I tell the boys at the base I was hit by a blind driver?"

Bean Pole (Homer) went to work in a piano factory in New York to get a better understanding of the repair of pianos. While there he apprenticed for an organ maker for the same purpose. He was in New York for two years and later moved to Beaumont, Texas, to work for his old school friend. As soon as he realized that his friend had ethics different than his own, he left Texas for McAlester, Oklahoma. There were many churches with pipe organs and several colleges with pipe organs and several pianos within a day's drive from there. As Player pianos were popular at the time and they required more time to repair and tune than a regular piano, Homer's income was excellent. He did well there and within two years had saved enough to build himself a new home.

I was unable to graduate when I flunked Geometry. Without a high school diploma, college was not an option for me. So I tuned pianos, taught private lessons in both organ and piano, helped Papa in his office when his nurse was away. A friend told me about a job she'd heard about that needed a blind person. I applied and got that job ironing clothes on the recently introduced electric mangle. I ironed everything from men's shirts to bed sheets. I worked in the window of a department store in front of a sign that said, "If the new Everyday Mangle is safe for a blind lady to use, it's safe for you." That job lasted for about a month, until people became used to a "blind lady ironing on the Everyday Mangle."

By this time Papa was spending less and less time at home. Mama knew that he allowed his office nurse the space we lived in when we first came to Arjenta and he was very open to say, they "were driving in the country", or "we went to the circus," *they* and *we* meaning Papa and his office nurse.

Mama was lonely at this time. It was just the two of us in that great big house most of the time. All my sisters were married and lived away from home and when their babies started to arrive, Mama was again needed and useful. I continued living at home even after my first proposal of marriage. Mama and Papa wouldn't allow me to marry because they thought it would end my musical career. The Professor had impressed upon them that my talent was a rare gift and must be encouraged, which also meant that any activity that might detour my music must be discouraged. I had a good circle of friends at church and with my school friends whose homes had always been in the area, so I enjoyed my life to some extent. It was somewhat limited by not having any of my sisters at home so Mama and Papa decided they would borrow me a *sister*.

One of my friends from the young people's group at church was named Blanche Morgan. Her mother had died and after her father remarried, he sent Blanche into Little Rock to make her living. She was living in a rooming house when I met her, so Mama invited her to stay with us for the company she gave me, hoping I'd be more content and forget about marriage. She not only became another sister for me but another daughter for Mama. We had many of the same interests and we laughed a lot together. Although, she didn't play any music, she enjoyed and encouraged my music.

One day when a group of us young adults were on our way home from a church social, six of us dismounted the street-car a few blocks from home. As soon as I took that stretch from the bottom step to the street, I felt the elastic band that held my bloomers to my waist pop. My underwear loosened and began to slip down. I grabbed my hip with my hand, pressing my upper bloomer line as tightly as I could to keep them from falling to the ground and absolutely embarrassing me to death. As soon as I told Blanche what had happened she sent the men to walk ahead slowly, and "don't look back", as she grouped the ladies around me in a closed store doorway. Fortunately, one of the girls had a safety pin in the hem of her dress and allowed it to be commandeered for my bloomer patrol. My decency was protected with one small pin. After that, they had the pin silver plated and mounted in a frame to hang on the wall of my room.

On another Sunday after church, Blanche asked Papa if she and I could borrow his horse and buggy. Since she was raised on a farm she was totally comfortable with horses. She invited me to go to visit her Aunt Min who also lived in the country. Blanche said that her Aunt Min was a simple woman of very modest means who raised most of her own foodstuffs. She lived alone. When we arrived we went into her kitchen for a cup of coffee. As we sat at her table Aunt Min asked if I'd ever seen a horse. When I told her I hadn't she said for me to reach over my head. I did. We were sitting with our backs to an open window and her horse was just outside the house with his head actually sticking through the window directly above me. I was so surprised when I touched his head inside the kitchen that I pulled back sharply amidst a howl of laughter from Blanche and Aunt Min. They loved my reaction and I got to see first hand the horse's head, just where on his head the ears were located, his long nose and wide mouth. I had touched a horse before so I knew about their short fur and long coarse mane and tail but I couldn't have imagined what his head looked like until the experience in Aunt Min's kitchen.

"Do I dare look at his teeth? Will he bite me?" I asked.

"Aunt Min said, "I don't think so but let me be there with you," as she walked around the table to be next to the horse."

She told me to just use the soft pads of me fingers to separate his lips and I could then feel his teeth." They were bigger than I had expected and it was a thrill to see them.

Writing new music came naturally for me. I simply sat at the piano in a room alone, thinking about what was jolly or sad in my life at the time. The music flowed.

I received a marriage proposal from a regular beau about a year after I left school. Professor Trebing had such faith in my ability that Papa said with my "gift" I owed it to the world to continue to write for all to enjoy. If I got married and had a family, I'd be too busy to write. I regretted but accepted his decision.

In the meantime, Homer Hudlow established himself well in his tuning profession in a town in eastern Oklahoma, McAlester. Player pianos were very popular at the time and took more time to repair or tune than regular pianos. His income was solid and increasing. He had a home built for himself. We had stayed in touch through an occasional letter and at the annual school reunion. If he was able he always returned to Little Rock for that function and we saw each other at that time. He never spoke of marriage. For a long time I thought he was in love with me and I with him, but nothing of a permanent nature was ever said. It was over two years after the first proposal, Homer went directly to Papa and asked for my hand.

At every opportunity, I spoke of my hope and expectation of following my sisters into marriage and a family. By this time my sisters had given my parents three grandchildren. I think Papa realized that it was only a matter of time when I'd be asked to marry again. He and mama liked Homer. Homer shared my interest in music. He played the piano and several of the woodwind instruments. He sang. We shared so many friends, all from school. After Mama and Papa talked it over, Papa said "Yes."

The first journey we took together was on the train from Little Rock to Russellville, Arkansas so I could meet his family. His one brother, Charlie, still lived on the old home place with his father and mother. Two sisters and another brother lived in the general area of the old home place. Homer's father had homesteaded a plot of 99 acres outside of Russellville, around the small town of Morrilton and several of the remaining eleven children were in a traveling distance of the old homestead. The family turned out in force to meet our train. Homer's sixteen year old niece, May, said I was the most beautiful woman she had ever seen in her whole life when I stepped down from the train. Sister Anna continued to make my clothes so I wore a royal blue wool suit with a matching hat, both of which she had made. I'd been told that my shiny dark hair was silky and healthy looking. I wore glass eyes at that point in my life, chosen by Mama to most closely match the blue eye coloring of her own and my sisters.

The Hudlows were wonderful people and made me feel welcome

from the moment I stepped off the train. Several siblings were out of town or state and I couldn't meet them until our wedding. That was on January 1st, 1922. We were married in the blind school's chapel, the very site of our great triumph over the oppressive mind of the infamous "Black Widow." The Professor conducted the school choir in a choral number I had written and the entire Mendelssohn's Wedding Song. Grace Davenport played the organ.

Mama said I had always walked like a proud Indian Chief, standing tall and straight and that I was elegant in the ankle length, high necked gown of pale gray chiffon that Anna had made for me. Anna picked the color because it complimented my now black hair. The waist was gathered and the long sleeves gathered at the shoulders and shirred from the elbow to the wrist. I had no trail or veil. I carried the Bible that Mama's father had given her when she left the old country. A pink ribbon was tied around that Bible with a small sprig of greenery on top.

It was a time of joy but also sadness. I was so happy, ready to be on my own and away from all who had nurtured my every move. Mama cried because I was the last of her children to leave home, she said.

We moved right into Homer's two bedroom house in McAlester. It was all new and clean. I was surprised to find that I didn't really mind washing the dishes anymore. It seemed quite different now that I was in my own home.

My first child, Anna Frances was born on October 14, 1922, Grace Inger on March 13, 1925 and Nancy Edna on April 15, 1929.

Homer's business went very well for many years. We could afford household help when Anna Frances was born. The fall she started first grade, I was pregnant with Nancy. Morning sickness always accompanied my pregnancies so those early months were not very pleasant. One day Grace Inger wandered off to play when she heard two little boys playing across the street. She knew she was to stay in the yard but her usual playmate, her sister, was in school and so the temptation was more than she could bear. That was a big mistake. One of the boys put a lighted wooden match to her rompers and set her afire. The nice neighbor in the corner house said her "screams were more than the usual play."

She jumped down the four steps of her back porch and rolled Grace in the grass to put out the fire before carrying her home. The neighbor came into our house and put her onto my bed. She was crying. The neighbor told me the burns were serious and instructed me to call the doctor immediately. She then left. I needed to see for myself and of course, I could only see her burns if I felt them. I leaned over and examined her. Her burns were third degree, almost to the bone on her thigh and hip. As soon as I realized this I apparently fainted. I came to having fallen on top of Grace and her screams were ear-bursting.

The doctor arrived, cleaned and dressed her injuries by using Ungunteen salve directly on the burns and then covered that with sterile gauze. The doctor came several times a week to clean and re-dress her wounds. Even though he was a big help, her pain was so great it was very difficult for me to care for her at all without further hurting her. So Mama came to stay with us to help dress her burns, with my pregnancy and later the new baby. She stayed for a little over a year.

The early days of my marriage were good days. The only day I questioned the wisdom in my marrying and having children was when my child was critically burned. I reasoned that had I had two good eyes I could have possibly watched Grace more closely and not allow her out of our own yard.

Mama was so comforting at that time when she explained all the things children can get into when their parents had two good eyes. Most of the time I was able to accept her counsel but there were always those times when my spirits were down and I thought sorry for myself.

In the town I was in great demand for luncheons at women's clubs, church gatherings to present my new original music and to perform on either the piano or pipe organ. Homer used me to assist him when he tuned the big organs. I sat at the keyboard and struck the requested keys while Homer worked in the rows of pipes to correct their pitch.

Churches hired me as a substitute organist after we got through a pack of questions about exactly what hymns I knew and or in what keys I could play those tunes. Once they understood I was a professional, could play all the hymns and in any key, that I knew my way around the organ, and the organ and church literature, I was accepted. At least I was accepted, until a new church interviewed me for the next job. Then the process repeated itself. Forever, people couldn't understand people who are blind usually are only unable to see out of their eyes. Usually everything else works, including their brain, their other senses and their memory. Most often, particularly if they have had little or sight, they over-compensate for the loss of their eyes and develop their other senses far more keenly than otherwise.

The Great Depression was very difficult on us in eastern Oklahoma. Miners of coal struck and never re-opened. Gradually, the piano tuning stopped altogether for individual homes. Thank goodness most of the churches and colleges could still afford to have their instruments tuned and repaired. Homer had a nervous breakdown in 1935 and couldn't work. We had used almost all of our savings when one of my school mates who worked for the state of Oklahoma hired me for several jobs. Since the state penitentiary was in McAlester, I was hired to teach Braille to the inmates who had lost their sight after incarceration. I went inside the prison once a week for that job. At no time did I ever feel threatened for guards were always right there in the room with us. Although, I was always a little squeamish about the inmate who had murdered his wife, ground her up into and sold her as hamburger meat. I was told he was caught when someone found a finger-nail in their meat.

The other job was very rewarding. At this time of fiscal destitution, poor people in Oklahoma were not able to afford medical care. When an eye problem occurred they just waited. Many were losing their sight altogether because they waited until their sight was gone to get help. This problem was very troubling to the Health Department of the state so they hired me and a nurse-guide with a car. We had an area within a days drive around McAlester to speak at church meeting, grange meetings, clubs and any group of people who would listen to us. I spoke about my life as a blind person and I preformed either on an organ or the piano, whatever they had. Then the nurse spoke and offered to inspect any person's eyes, free of charge, who had any kind of eye problem at all. Many were referred to hospitals for surgery or to doctor's in state facilities for advanced treatment. Many people were saved from either complete blindness or further deterioration of the eyesight.

I felt good about that job, realizing it was a great help to many people. It was a god-send for my family since my husband didn't work and we had no income except what I could provide. Women didn't work then. For any jobs available the men were used so I was very grateful to have a friend from school who remembered me for the job when it became available.

Homer had bought me a fine grand piano and when my children were sick or just tired, they would ask me to play them "to sleep." They each had their own favoritesas did their father and our friends. We had many good family times with me playing the piano, Homer on his saxophone, and the girls lined behind by size to parade in a circle snaking through the inside of the house. Many a supper ended with the marches and singing. Everyone in the family sang, just like when I was a small child at home in Council Bluffs and at the gatherings in Mama's family. Like the quartets my sisters and mother would sing our little family sang with my piano accompaniment by all our lives.

All my girls were musical. All three studied piano. In addition, Anna played the violin and sang, Grace the French Horn, harp and sang, and Nancy the violin, saxophone and oboe. All played in symphony orchestras at sometime during their lifetimes. After my girls grew up and had their own families and the family gathered for birthdays and holidays, our family sang together. While Mama was alive the sing-fest always sang in six or seven part harmony with all the men and the cousins joining in. Each time we concluded in a beautiful but tearful rendition of Malotte's Lord's Prayer.

My girls played the same games that my sister's played with me when we were growing up, selecting between one of the bodies before me, or the trees or buildings.

All my stories and songs were repeated a thousand times, even in the porch swing on warm summer evenings when my grandchildren were visiting. Homer relied on my memory as he referred to me as his "walking telephone directory." As his hearing diminished in his older years, he needed my strong sense of hearing and fine memory. Of course, he was often my *EYES*. But that was frequently reversed when in his older years he misplaced his eye glasses or his keys. I was always able to find them for him.

The last visit with my old friend, Blanche and sister, Inger, both in their 80's, one had lost her direct, straight forward sight and the other had lost her peripheral vision. I could thread their needles for them. I took the lead when we went out together, one on each arm to guide them around. I told them when the curbs were coming up for I knew the block sizes and when to expect the end. I was used to it. They broke up in laughter at my declaration, "Ladies, the blind IS now leading the blind."